SEND IN HIS CLOWNS

A workshop manual for training clown ministers

by
STEPHEN P. PERRONE
& JAMES P. SPATA

Meriwether Publishing Ltd., Publisher
P.O. Box 7710
Colorado Springs, CO 80933

Designer: Michelle Zapel
Photographer: Ted Zapel
Executive Editor: Arthur Zapel
Manuscript Editor: Kathy Pijanowski

ISBN: 0-916260-32-1
© Copyright MCMLXXXV Meriwether Publishing Ltd.
Printed in the United States of America
First Edition

ACKNOWLEDGEMENTS

There are so many kind people who have been helpful and encouraging in the writing of this book. We are especially thankful to Judy Walther and Nancy Fees for their ingenuity and tireless hours in helping us develop this workshop. A debt is owed to Paul and Barbara Humphries, who first trained us in clown ministry, and to the young people of the Episcopal Diocese of Long Island and their leaders, who have been our guinea pigs in developing and perfecting this workshop. Finally, we thank our families, who have been so kind and supportive in the time needed to develop this workshop.

TABLE OF CONTENTS

Chapter 1

BECOMING FOOLS FOR CHRIST

From a letter written by a clown to God:

❝ *When a man becomes a clown, he makes a free gift of himself to his audience. To endow them with the saving grace of laughter, he submits himself to being mocked, drenched, clouted, crossed in love. Your Son made the same submission when He was crowned as a mock king and the troops spat wine and water in His face . . . My hope is that when He comes again, He will still be human enough to shed a clown's gentle tears over the broken toys that were once your children.* **❞** [1]

So, you've seen some clowns and it looked like fun. You get some make-up and a silly suit — but then, what? The Barnum and Bailey organization spends $10,000 and up to six weeks of intensive training to produce a beginning clown (they walk behind the elephants with a broom). There must be more to it than seems evident on the surface.

"The clown is not simply a painted face and colorful costume that moves clumsily in parody of a human being." [2] He or she is a mirror reflecting the joy, the fault, the absurd in the world around him or her.

The Christian clown is not a new or even a radical concept. However, we live in a particularly conservative era, so a concept which equates the role of a white-faced fool dressed in colorful rags with the ministry of the church seems radical. In ministry as clowns, we have found rejection from those whose concepts are inflexible and theologically joyless. For most, however, the clown, whether a part of the liturgy, or found in hospital, church fair or on the street, is a source of joy and opportunity — opportunity to get beyond the problems and pressures in our all-too-serious world.

There is a warning on the label of this package we call "Clown Ministry." It reads, *"This ministry is exhausting, both physically and mentally."*

[1] West, Morris, *The Clowns of God* (William Morrow & Co., Inc.).

[2] Sanders, Toby, *How to Be a Complete Clown*, copyright 1979 Toby Sanders. Reprinted with permission of Stein and Day Publishers.

An expenditure of time and resources is required, and you must be prepared for rejection as well as acceptance. With that warning, let us tell you that it can be one of the most heady experiences in the ministry of our Lord Jesus Christ.

If you can imagine bringing a smile to the face of a broken and frightened youngster stuck for weeks in a hospital bed; or wiping the tears of joy and love from the face of a senior citizen who sees nothing ahead but the scythe of the grim reaper; then read on, for "fools for Christ" may be for you.

Becoming a clown minister is a joy — a joy in the context of prayer, study and service — the tripod of Christian life and renewal. As clown ministers, getting outside our personal history and psychology is the first and most important sacrifice we make. We can tell you, from personal experience, that success as a clown minister is directly equatable to a personal willingness to give up static and preconceived notions of how God's people are served.

Our clown ministry on Long Island happens to be an organization without charter or meetings. There are no dues or officers. (There are clown organizations you may want to join. Some of them are listed in the resources section, Chapter XIII.) We are dedicated to minister to God's people as clowns. Clowns come in all types, and we do not say it shall be thus and no other. We do share with you the way we do it; use, adapt, change and direct it to fit your needs and your concept of the Christian clown.

Clown ministry is catechesis, a word used to describe *"all those activities of a community by which both individuals and community are led to a deeper faith."* [3] We are caught in a world which places a high value on secular humanism, which keys in on individuals apart from the context of the faith community. The more knowledge we gain, however, the more important we find the Spirit and the community of the faithful. Often, theology has become a theoretical trip into an intellectual nirvana, disembodied from the mainstream of truth. The clown can be an integrator, for he/she brings love in humility to this broken and sinful world.

In some small way, the clown is a paradigm of Christ in the community. He/she transports others to a time and a place where joy is real and love encompasses all, even when that time is not within the lifetime of those to whom he/she ministers.

The clown is an artist, one who needs to be disciplined and skilled, for clowning done poorly will in no way achieve the ends for which it is designed.

[3] Warren, Michael, *Youth and the Future of the Church*, copyright 1982 Michael Warren (Minneapolis: Winston/ Seabury Press). Formerly published by The Seabury Press. All rights reserved. Used by permission.

Our goal is to produce a clown minister. This workshop is a start, but only a start. You and your troupe have a lifetime of perfecting yet ahead of you.

For this reason, we ask that you do not use the clown ministry workshop as a program-filler for some activity period when it just happens to fit perfectly. Accept this ministry as an ongoing ministry and provide opportunities for your troupe of clowns to minister, to sharpen their skills, and to indeed become "fools for Christ." We suggest such facilities as nursing homes, hospitals and shopping malls, and such events as local parades, schools, parish picnics, fairs, etc., as ideal laboratories.

The workshop we describe in the subsequent pages takes about nine hours and a crew of at least four facilitators. Several hours of advanced planning is also essential to the successful completion of this workshop. Try not to run a workshop with any more than 25 people, including participants and facilitators.

We wish you all success and blessings in this ministry, and ask your prayers in our efforts for our Lord.

Chapter 11

PLANNING THE WORKSHOP

The success of your workshop depends in large part on preparation. Homework and advanced planning ensure a smooth operation. Advertising, preparation of the various parts of the workshop, decisions on logistics and even preparation of songs and music allow us to fit into nine hours a workshop that could easily take three days. In your planning, you might seek help from people in your community who are experts in circus arts and skills. (It's surprising how many of them are around.) If you use the workshop as a conference weekend or an extended experience, make sure to adapt the schedule which follows to fit the available time, and to break at logical points. With much planning and some additional preparation in mime, history and circus skills such as juggling, tumbling, balancing and acrobatics, a semester course could be developed from the material.

Please do not try to "wing it." The material in this manual works, but it cannot have its full impact if you do not prepare well in advance.

Here is a list of points to remember in your preparations:

1. Pray!

2. Advertising: Prepare flyers and other advertising several weeks in advance. (A sample flyer is found at the end of the chapter.) Make sure that you have advance registration, because materials are expensive, and the workshop becomes unwieldy with more than about 20 participants. We advise a short meeting with participants prior to the workshop experience to explain the nature of the ministry and to explain that the workshop is only the first step in what can become a lifetime ministry.

3. Facilitators: This workshop is not for heroes. Don't try to do it alone. The workshop is exhausting, and in the long run, your running a solo show would be unfair to the participants. The workshop works best with a facilitating team of three or four. A team meeting or two prior to the workshop would be helpful in developing timing and understanding. During these meetings, decide what each facilitator will do, set up the workshop schedule and assign advance planning tasks.

4. **Materials:** Obtain all materials needed for the workshop. (A list follows this section.) The initial monetary outlay is high, but many of the materials (such as make-up) can be used for quite a while. The facilitators should decide how the materials are to be paid for (church treasury, group funds, workshop fees, cake sales, car washes, etc.). Some materials are needed only for the workshop and not for future ministry. Check to see whether these materials can be borrowed from Sunday school or other sources. This kind of planning will help keep the costs down.

5. **Facility:** Study the area where the workshop will be held. Determine logistics and decide in advance how movement will take place. Decide how you will handle any meals or snacks.

6. **Participants:** They should be fully aware of what they are expected to bring with them; i.e., clown costume, mirror, brown-bag lunch, etc.

7. **Paperwork:** Prepare blank clown faces and graduation certificates for the workshop. Samples of these forms are at the end of this chapter. Please use them, if you wish, or design your own forms.

8. **Camera:** An instant film-developing camera (Polaroid or Kodak) is useful in preparing certificates at the end of the workshop. This kind of camera should not be too difficult to borrow. Pictures are taken in full make-up and costume. Have a jar or stick of glue available so you can affix each individual's picture to his/her certificate.

9. **Practical Exercise:** Make all arrangements in advance for the practical exercise which ends the training session. Call a hospital, nursing home, health-related facility or similar institution. Arrange to spend about an hour there with the clown troupe. (Make sure to integrate your workshop schedule and the time arranged with the institution.) It is essential that your trainees have an opportunity to minister and to experience this servant ministry first-hand. By some, this is called "taking the plunge!" Do not neglect this important bit of preparation, even if it's simply a trip to a nearby park or playground.

A note of caution: we have found nursing facilities to be notorious for passing the buck. Make sure you know the name of the person you contact and his or her position. Be certain who will be there personally when you arrive. *And* confirm your arrangements as often as you feel comfortable, so that your troupe does not come in cold off the street to be greeted with an unfriendly unwelcome!

10. **Transportation:** Make sure all transportation arrangements are made in advance. Cars will be loaded with anxious and somewhat "hyper" clowns. Drivers should be selected who can deal with this situation.

11. **Closing Service:** Any special planning necessary for the closing service should be made in advance. If a priest or minister is required, make sure there is one available.

12. **Clean-up:** Make advance plans for clean-up. After nine hours of instruction and ministry, you will appreciate help in packing it all up and cleaning the facility. Once again, this is not a place for heroism.

13. **Pray!**

WORKSHOP MATERIALS

- we recommend posters of clowns, balloons, etc., to decorate the facility where the workshop is held
- ball or other object to talk to (See Chapter IV.)
- song books or printed song sheets
- blackboard, newsprint or poster paper
- crayons and clown-face blanks
- book or movie version of *The Clown of God* by Tomie de Paola (Refer to chapters VI and XIII.)
- lunch (if brown-bag, be sure to notify participants)
- props for clowning
- make-up needs:

  - mirrors (Make sure participants bring their own.)

  - heavy sock(s) filled with talcum powder

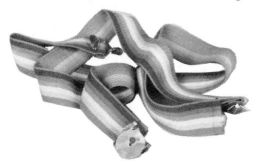

- clown white (12-ounce can) grease paint
- cotton swabs
- red and black grease paint (several sticks or tubes of each)
- soft (babies') hair brushes
- squirt bottle
- make-up brushes (minimum three for each color)
- red and black grease pencils
- cold cream, Albelene or vegetable shortening (cheaper and just as effective) for make-up removal
- paper towels (Make sure there is enough for making up and for make-up removal.)

● balloons, pompons, etc. (to use as hand-outs)

● felt-tipped markers

● extra costume materials (Each participant is asked to bring his/her own costume materials, but there is always someone who has forgotten, or has no costume in mind prior to the workshop.)

● diplomas (See the sample at the end of this chapter.)

● camera, film and flash bulbs (preferably the "instant" type of camera process — pictures are attached to the diploma and given out at the end of the workshop)

● tape recorder or record player and desired pieces of material for the faith imagination meditations (chapters V and X)

● all needs for closing service (Chapter XII)

WORKSHOP SCHEDULE

This workshop schedule is meant as a guide. It can be incorporated into an overnight retreat program, split into two successive four- or five-hour sessions, or accomplished in one single nine-hour block. We have always relied on lots of Christian music to act as transitions and to mark rest times in the course of the workshop.

- **8:30 a.m.**　　team assembles for preparation and prayer
- **9:00 a.m.**　　songs, ice-breakers (Chapter III), coffee, doughnuts
- **9:30 a.m.**　　expectation exercises (Chapter IV)
- **9:45 a.m.**　　songs
- **10:00 a.m.**　　"Clown Tag" (Chapter IV)
- **10:15 a.m.**　　"Meet My Clown" meditation (Chapter V)
- **10:45 a.m.**　　debriefing — sharing reactions
- **11:00 a.m.**　　sketching clowns; juice and cookies
- **11:30 a.m.**　　songs
- **11:45 a.m.**　　clown history (Chapter VI)
- **12:05 p.m.**　　story: *Clown of God*
- **12:30 p.m.**　　lunch
- **1:00 p.m.**　　pantomime (Chapter VII)
- **1:30 p.m.**　　the ministry of the Christian clown (Chapter VIII)
- **2:10 p.m.**　　tools of the clown minister (Chapter IX)
- **2:30 p.m.**　　meditation on whiteface (Chapter X)
- **2:50 p.m.**　　making up (Chapter XI)
- **3:30 p.m.**　　practical exercise (Chapter XII)
- **5:00 p.m.**　　closing service
- **5:30 p.m.**　　clean-up
- **6:00 p.m.**　　departure

SAMPLE REGISTRATION FORM

WHEN:
SATURDAY,
MARCH 9TH
9:00 A.M. -
6:00 P.M.

WHERE:
CHRIST'S
CHURCH

COST: $3

BRING YOUR
LUNCH

REGISTRATION FORM

NAME: _____

I plan to attend "Clown Saturday" at Christ's church.
Enclosed is my $3 registration fee. I will bring with me a
mirror, clown costume and my lunch.

_____
(sign here)

SAMPLE DIPLOMA

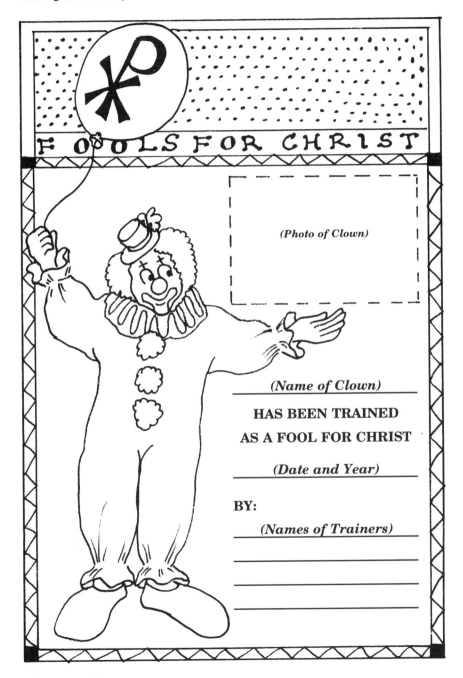

FOOLS FOR CHRIST

(Photo of Clown)

(Name of Clown)

**HAS BEEN TRAINED
AS A FOOL FOR CHRIST**

(Date and Year)

BY:

(Names of Trainers)

ICE-BREAKERS

Here are some activities that we have used as ice-breakers and getting-in-touch exercises. They will help to relax the group and help its members get to know each other a little better. You are certainly not restricted to the examples on the following pages, but may use any exercise that promotes fellowship and relaxes the participants. Books devoted to these types of exercises are available. Some of the better-known are listed in Chapter XlII.

The Magic Ball

Using a ball, a doll or some other object (we've even used a cola bottle):

1. **Have the participants think about the following:** "If l could be anything l wanted in the world, what would it be?" Encourage imagination and wit. Examples:

   - an ant playing "Dixie" on a Sousaphone

   - a wave licking the shoreline

   - a rainbow

   - a kiss on a mother's lips

   - a frog on a lily pad

   - a hippopotamus in a tutu

   - a ladybug on the Empire State Building

   - an eagle in a chicken coop

2. **Form a circle.**

3. **Starting with one of the facilitators, each should say:** "I am (first name), and I want to be _____ ."
Pass the magic ball to the next person on the right or left. That person then says: "I am _____ ,
and I want to be _____ ; and
he/she is _____ , and he/she
wants to be _____ ."

Remember to explain that the magic ball will remember everything that is said, but you need to talk to it and look at it for help. Continue around the circle, introducing everyone who has previously been introduced, until the last person has to introduce the entire circle.

Puzzle Cards

In order to break down into small groups:

1. **Obtain several Christmas or birthday cards,** or other kinds of picture cards.

2. **Cut the cards into eight jigsaw-type pieces.**

3. **Shuffle all the cards together.**

4. **Distribute the pieces** and have participants find their group by finding the picture to which their pieces belong.

Knots

Break the group down into units of about eight each.

1. **Have units form a circle.**

2. **Have each person grab the hand of two other people in the circle,** making sure that neither of the others was standing next to him/her. He/she must not be holding both hands of any one person.

3. **Without them breaking their grip, let each unit's members**

untangle themselves until they have formed a circle. (Sometimes, the unit will form two separate circles; sometimes, a figure eight.) You might wish to do this as a race.

In addition to exercises of this type, we have found music to be an excellent ice-breaker. Songs like "I've Got the Joy," "Rise and Shine" or "Give Me Oil in My Lamp" are fun to sing, and singing is an easy way of getting everyone to participate.

As the day goes on, we try to incorporate more serious songs into the workshop that help reinforce the theme of a particular block of study. The song that follows, "Let Me Be Your Servant," was written for our workshops by one of our clown facilitators.

LET ME BE YOUR SERVANT

Words by
Betty Palkingham
Music by
Nancy Fees

2. I will weep when you are weeping. When you laugh, I'll laugh with you.
   I'll share your joy and sorrow 'til we've seen this journey through.
   When we sing to God in heaven, we shall find such harmony,
   born of all we've known together, of Christ's love and agony. *(To Refrain)*

Chapter IV:

EXPECTATION EXERCISES

After the warm-up activities (songs and/or ice-breaker games), the initial expectation exercises are begun. These exercises are designed for two purposes.

The first of these purposes is to develop a sense that the expectations of the group are not really very clear and that there is a general willingness to take the day as it unfolds.

We use this approach to accomplish this purpose. Ask the participants why they came to the workshop and what they expect to gain from participating. Ask the question of the group as a whole. Record the results on a sheet of poster paper or newsprint or on a blackboard. Leave this in plain view and refer back to it during the final exercises of the workshop. Resist the temptation to editorialize during the exercise. Simply record everyone's expectations.

The second purpose of these exercises is for the participants to sense the profound nature of the clown as a minister.

Have a blackboard or newsprint easel available to record the responses. Keep them on display throughout the workshop. Divide the writing surface into two halves, left and right. On the left-hand column, write at the top, "A CLOWN IS . . . "

Appoint a scribe to write down *all* the responses you receive when you ask the question. Some of the images of a clown will be profound, some will be whimsical, and some may even be painful, but write them down, regardless.

When you think you've exhausted the possible responses, move on to the second part of the exercise. (We try to elicit at least one observation from every participant at the workshop.)

Write at the top of the right-hand column, "JESUS IS . . .", in very large letters. This is to show the true servant nature of the ministry of the clown. A period of silence should be kept to allow time for the participants to integrate this analogy.

This exercise should take no longer than 15 minutes. When completed, sing a few songs as a bridge to the next activity, which is playing "Clown Tag."

The game starts as a regular game of tag. The rules are only that one foot must be on the floor at all times, and that you say, "You're it!" when you have tagged someone. There are no tag-backs. Run the regular tag about two or three minutes, then switch to slow tag.

In slow tag, everything is done in slow motion — even your speech. You tag someone, saying, "You'rrrre iiittttttt!" Make all motions deliberate and exaggerated. This is a good introduction to miming, and makes a good practice exercise. Continue slow tag for about two or three minutes. (This provides facilitators with needed rest.) Then switch to fast tag.

In fast tag, body motions are speeded up, but the floor speed is not. Again, motions should be exaggerated; shuffling feet, speeded-up arm motions and rapid, high-pitched speech should characterize this exercise. Continue this for three or four minutes. Participants should be winded if they are doing this portion of the exercise properly.

Chapter V

A FACE TO STOP A THOUSAND TEARS

This is a faith imagination exercise. Faith imagining, or dynamic imagining, is a concept and technique which allows the imagination, latent in most of us, to break free and focus vivid pictures on the conscious mind. It is a very freeing technique which releases untapped energies. Training in dynamic imagining can be useful not only in clown ministry, mime and acting, but can be used with scripture study, in healing ministries and in mental health care.

Imagining is a powerful way of releasing the energies of the mind in a focused way. We do the same thing in an uncontrolled manner when we daydream. When cultivated, imagining can bend the principles of probability in a particular direction. Seeing yourself as a clown can, in time, make you a master of the art. Seeing yourself whole, forgiven, healed or loved can produce a conformity of mind and body to that estate.

This first exercise in dynamic imagining is an elementary one. In it, we attempt to open the world of imagination to a generation that is starved for such stimulation. Initially, there may be some discomfort. Use the relaxation exercise to provide this settling-down time before the actual imagining is attempted.

Make sure you are thoroughly familiar with this kind of exercise before you try it. The exercise will not work if you simply read the contents of these pages to your participants. Use a soothing monotone voice so that participants can reach deep within their imaginations. You will have to fit the exercise to the group as far as length and intensity is concerned.

Faith imagining can be unpredictable and even dangerous if you are not careful. Remember, you are releasing the power of the mind and freeing the imagination. Be prepared for some powerful reactions, especially from adults.

Dr. Norman Vincent Peale's book, *Dynamic Imaging,* [1] is a good instruction for the facilitator who will lead this exercise.

[1] Peale, Dr. Norman Vincent, *Dynamic Imaging.* (New York: Guidepost Press, 1980)

Relaxation

Have participants lie on the floor immediately after playing Clown Tag. They will be winded and tense. Make sure they have enough room so they can spread out comfortably. (Ask them to fully extend their arms. If they touch someone, they should move.) Go through a series of muscle tense-relax exercises. Starting with the toes, have them curl them as hard as possible for 15 seconds and then release the tension. Instruct the participants to concentrate on each part of the body as they go. Move from the toes to the feet to the ankles to the calves, etc., until you get to the shoulders, alternately tensing and relaxing the various parts. Once you reach the shoulders, start at the fingers and work back up to the shoulders, neck and head.

Now have them close their eyes and concentrate only on your voice. They are to let their bodies sink into a cloud — a soft, billowy, pink cloud. They are to relax and enjoy and listen to the voice.

Imagination Exercise

Go right into this exercise from the relaxation cloud. Let it flow smoothly and naturally. Don't worry about details; we change them each time we do it. Do have a tape of circus music available. We begin with stage-setting.

Sample monologue:

You are walking down a road. See the road ahead of you. Feel the road. Feel the warmth of the sun. See the trees and grass. Smell the freshness of the air. Hear the birds. It's so nice, so peaceful. Oh, look at the tree over there. Isn't it lovely? Look — there's a fence off to your right. See it there? Look at the field beyond the fence — it's so inviting that it seems to call. Hop over the fence. Feel the grass under your feet. Doesn't that smell good? Look at those little flowers. Aren't they pretty? The sun feels so nice and warm. It's such a nice day. *(Start music softly.)*

Oh, what's that? Where's that music coming from? It's over that little hill, there. Go on and climb up the hill. *(The music gets louder.)* The music is so inviting. You crest the hill, and there, in the valley on the other side, you see it — a circus tent — red and white stripes, a flag flying on the top. It's the big top *(music should be clear and loud)*, and there, down in front of the tent, you see someone. It's — it's a clown. How exciting! Wow!

You start down the hill. You run faster and faster, and as you run, the clown runs toward you. You meet — panting, breathless. You embrace. There is something very special about this clown. You look at each other — how beautiful. Look at the clown. How does the clown look? See the face — the features, the person. With your arms around each other, dance, romp, enjoy. And now — and now for a little magic.

Let go of the clown. Go around behind the clown. You didn't see it before, but there's a big zipper right down the back of the clown. Unzip the zipper. Go ahead; it's OK. Unzip the zipper and climb inside — become the clown!

Dance — dance, clown, dance. Feel the freedom and, because you're a magic clown, fly free and light. Soar, clown. Zoom and fly. You're free. Circle the flag over the big top. Fly loops and dives. Climb and whirl — free — wonderfully, marvelously free — free like the wind. Up, down, round and around. Fly. Enjoy. *(Slow down.)* What a feeling!

Uh, slow down now; slow down and approach the ground. There you are, back on the ground, but the freedom remains — the joy — the exhilaration deep inside. The time has come to leave. Unzip the clown. Climb out. Zip the clown back up. Go round front. Look at the clown again. Hug your clown. Look into the clown's face. Look deeply. Hug the clown.

Now turn — it's time to leave. Climb the hill. Look longingly back. Wave to the clown. Start down the other side of the hill. There's a bit of heaviness in your step, but inside, the excitement stays. Walk across the field. There's the fence. Climb back over the fence. Head back up the road. It's time to return. Slowly bring yourself back, and as you are ready, open your eyes.

Post-Experience

Once everyone has opened his/her eyes, or after about two minutes, start the group sharing experiences. Don't exceed 10 minutes in this segment. Participants may talk more freely if they are broken up into groups of three or four people.

My Clown

Explain to the participants that the clown they met during the exercise was, in fact, their own clown, and that in order to begin to get in touch with who that clown is, the participants should sketch the clown they saw. We hand out the Clown Face Blanks to each participant (see the samples at the end of the chapter), and crayons are made available.

Although the clown envisioned may be very elaborate and ornate, simplicity is the best way to go today. There will be time in the future to develop the clown. In fact, many professional circus clowns have taken years to develop their character. Also explain that participants may have seen other colors on their clowns, but that for this exercise and for the workshop today, they will be limited to the use of only red and black.

CLOWN FACE BLANK
(Front View)

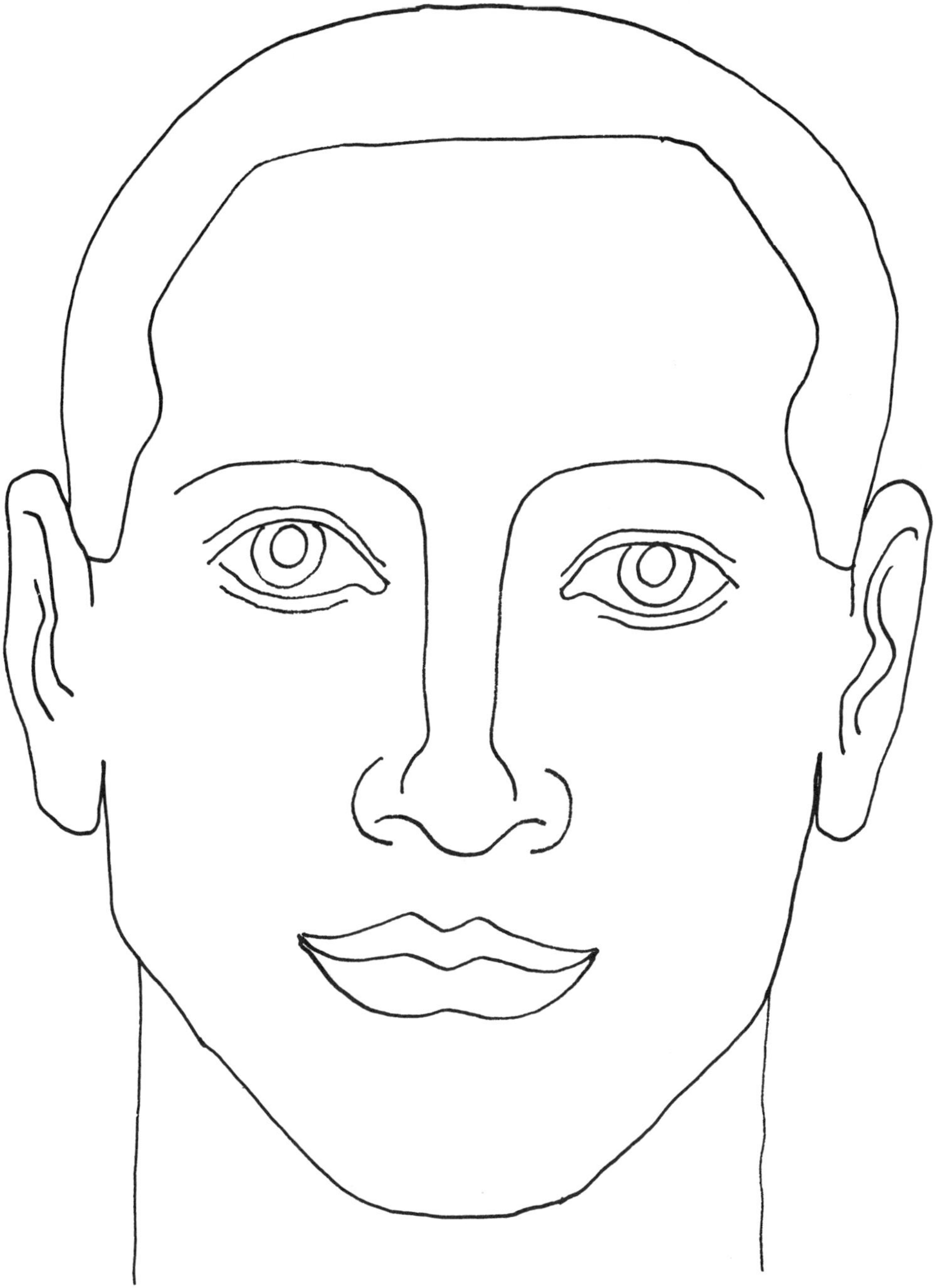

CLOWN
FACE
BLANK
(Side View)

Chapter VI:

CLOWN HISTORY

This brief look at the history of clowning is useful for the workshop because it gives the participants some insight into the different approaches one can find in clowning and helps define the clown character that is developing for each person.

The art and origin of the clown are lost in history. The clown has changed form and role in time, place and culture; but the clown has remained the safety valve of mankind throughout history. The ability to laugh — and especially to laugh at oneself — sets civilized beings apart from the wild beast. The clown makes fun out of failure, joy out of sadness, levity out of pain.

The word *clown* comes from the Anglo-Saxon *clod* — a lump of dirt; the lowest, the most common. And this is what the clown is called to be: the slave of all; the lowest, clumsiest, most foolish.

St. Paul writes, *"Let no one deceive himself. If anyone among you thinks he is wise in this age, let him become a fool that he may be wise."* (1 Corinthians 3:18) The God clown, the Jesus fool — this is what we seek to be. To become the person with no power, the lowly one who does the commonest job and the most menial task; this is our longing, our aim. Aspiring clowns for Barnum and Bailey begin their training with a broom and a shovel and walk behind the elephants. In our ministry, Jesus is our example. He was mocked, beaten, hung naked in death on a cross:

❝ Behold . . . the poorest king who ever lived. Before my creatures, I stand stripped, the cross my death-bed . . . even this is not my own. ❞ [1]

And what about the clown's white face? Whiteface is the universal sign of death. Peoples throughout the world as well as time have used white (pigment, ashes, crushed stone, plant juice, etc.) to signify death.

But why clowns? Why do clowns use the death mask? The reason is

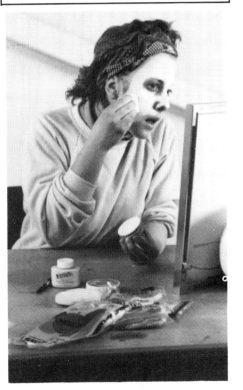

[1] Enzler, Clarence, *Everyman's Way to the Cross* (Notre Dame: Ave Maria Press, 1970). Used with permission of the publisher. All rights reserved.

simple, yet profound. The clown laughs at pain, at humiliation, at all the mockery and insult the world can bring to bear. And the clown says, "You can't hurt me; you can't humiliate me; you can't embarrass me; you can't even kill me! You see, I'm already dead!"

It is amazing to see what this transformation achieves in the lives of the clowns. We have seen person after person put on whiteface and leave behind timidity, fear, reputation, position — everything they hold sacred — and for that time (often the first in their lives), be a fool in the service of Christ.

We would like to share with you some of the twists and turns that have occurred along "clown alley."

The oldest records we have of clowns are of the cavorting street mimes shown in hieroglyphics on the walls of Egyptian and Cretan tombs. They were slapstick clowns whose antics entertained and amused the people.

Royal courts have always been places of intensity and great serious-ness because of the weighty matters of state. It is in just such a place that the role of the fool, the jester, is most vital. These clowns dressed in colorful rags ornamented with bells and rattles, and they often carried a puppet or the jawbone of an ass. Besides the funny, zany stories and crazy antics designed to amuse and entertain the court, they often presented profound insights in ways that were acceptable to those who had to make the weighty decisions of state. Pranks were often played on members of the court to remind them that in spite of their royal office, they were people, and ought to look at how seriously they take themselves.

In the Middle Ages, clowns were often used in worship — especially in large cathedrals. Because of the remoteness of the altar and the length of the services, the clown would often draw attention to a particular action or remind the worshipers of some truth of the faith.

The clown has always had a place in worship, reminding us of the folly of the creature trying to present anything to God, the author and creator of all. We must never underestimate the importance of this ministry in the church. We hope that the clowns in our midst, in and out of make-up, will deliver us from the arrogance with which we often approach our worship.

What about our modern clown? What are his origins? To find our modern clown, we must look at the traveling *commedia dell'artes* of Renaissance Europe. These troupes of strolling players toured Europe for several centuries. They worked town squares and country fairs as well as the houses of the nobility, and they gathered audiences wherever they could. They had stock characters, and they used the personalities of these characters to develop comedy routines. Clowns became vital to the non-stop entertainments the *commedia* offered. They filled in between the acts; performed to cover the prop people and the roustabouts as they changed the scenery; and drew attention to the main attractions. Eventually, the clowns, as well as other directors of attention, became lenses through which people could see themselves in a true comic context.

So you see, the clowns did not have their start in circuses, which is where we principally picture them today.

The clowns of today's tradition are of two general types. The first is descended from the Harlequin character of the *commedia*. This clown's face is white, his/her nose is red, and a baggy outfit covers his/her padded body. This is the master clown, a schemer, always devising means of getting others in trouble without getting in trouble himself/herself. These clowns are always silent, using mime and props to convey their antics.

The second type of clown is the "Auguste" (from the German, "clumsy boy"). There are many stories about the origin of this clown. The most widely known is the story of Tom Belling.

Tom was a rider in the Remy Circus of Berlin in the 1860s. One day, Tom was trying on the oversized pants of one of the stable hands. He was discovered by the ill-tempered owner of the show, who chased Tom about the grounds. While Tom ran blindly trying to escape the blows of the irate owner, he stumbled into the center ring. He kept running, trying to remove the pants at the same time. The audience roared at this hilarious antic. It was so well-received that the owner included it as a regular feature of the show.

The clumsy Auguste has a pink (or sometimes unshaven-looking) face, exaggerated features and outlandish props. He/she is always bumbling and stumbling, attempting to be helpful, but always getting into trouble in the process. The Auguste is often the butt of the whiteface's schemes. Most character clowns have evolved from this tradition. Among the great modern character clowns are Emmett Kelly and Charlie Chaplin. Auguste clowns sometimes use their voices, but this is by no means universal.

The great showman P.T. Barnum said that *"clowns are pegs to hang a circus on."* For many years, clowning outside of the circus was considered taboo. Today, however, we see a resurgence of the clown in contexts other than the circus; they take the forms of street mimes, character clowns in advertisements and markets, clowns at parties, in movies, and in shows like *Godspell*. We are starting to see the clown again take his/her place as society's toy. The clown has also re-emerged as the church fool, a minister bringing the joy of Christ.

In church as well as out, the clown is the servant, the sacrifice and the redeemer from all the cares and pressures of this all-too-serious world.

Lou Jacobs, one of today's great character clowns, writes:

66 When I put on my clown costume, I step through a magic door and become part of a sacred profession. All my make-up, baggy pants, funny hats, gay-colored scarves and floppy shoes are just the things I wear. The best part comes from inside me. Every clown knows that real success arrives only when you give of yourself to other people. Then they will become happy and laugh with you. 99

We like to end our discussion of the history of clowning by reading a story that has been adapted from a legend which began to be circulated during the Renaissance. The story is called *The Clown of God* and is written by Tomie de Paola. The reason we have used this piece is that it integrates the history and theology of clowning, and at the same time, it is an emotional preparation for the remainder of the workshop. We strongly advise that you read beforehand whatever you will use in this slot. It is often a shock when you find yourself in tears while reading children's books. *Clown of God* is also available in a 16-minute film distributed by Winston Woods and is available through many public library services. We have found showing the film or reading the story to be a very important part of the preparation for the actual experience of clowning, because it encourages participants to give all that they can, to consider their lives secondary.

Some other resources helpful in this regard might be Shel Silverstein's *Giving Tree; The Velveteen Rabbit*, by Margery Williams; or *The Little Prince*, by Antoine de Saint Exupery. Another film, *The Juggler of Notre Dame*, released by Paulist Press, is very effective if you extend the workshop (this film runs about 45 minutes). Other appropriate stories may be used.

Chapter VII:

MIME EXERCISES

Our clown ministry is a *silent* ministry. We convey our messages by gesture and interplay. We therefore need to take some time to develop pantomime skills. Obviously, the half-hour put aside in the nine-hour schedule is hardly enough time for anything other than a cursory introduction to mime.

Therefore, the mimes we develop in this workshop will be unsophisticated. You should not be satisfied to leave mime at this point, and should consider an advanced workshop to work at these clowning skills at some later date.

Mime skills have little to do with body type or even dexterity. There are mimes which can be developed for each person. The clown minister must learn to use the body to its greatest advantage and select mime movements which fit the person best. (If you are tall and broad, you might try to smell flowers or jump rope, or cower in fear of a tiny dog. If you are small and petite, you might consider battling a windmill, or playing football with a group of gorillas, emerging victorious.)

Miming does not express words; instead, it communicates thoughts and emotions. These feelings are expressed through the gestures and the eyes of the clown. He/she sees what isn't there, acts upon what he/she sees, and does it in such a way that the audience sees it, too! [1] Our exercises should, therefore, stress the use of gestures and facial expressions.

The exercises may be done all at once as suggested in the schedule, or scattered throughout the workshop. Some time needs to be given after the participants are in make-up to create mime exercises in their clown character.

Mime requires a sensitivity to the essential motions of any particular task. These motions are usually exaggerated and emphasized. It would be very helpful to the participants if the facilitators demonstrate a number of simple mime exercises. If they are prepared well, the students will gain

[1] Litherland, Janet, *The Clown as Minister* (Colorado Springs, Colorado: Meriwether Publishing Ltd., Contemporary Drama Service, 1981).

confidence and self-assurance from the performances.

Explain the importance of the sacredness of another person's space. As clown ministers, we must never invade like a center-stage performer, but rather invite and entice others into our space. As a clown minister, your space must be open and free for others to choose to enter and leave at will. The spectator may, in fact, choose not to enter at all, and the clown minister should be prepared for this initial rejection.

In mime, the eyes are always the conveyor of intent. The clown minister's eyes, therefore, must say, "yes," "come," "I love," "I care." If eye contact is impossible, the spectator has probably chosen not to enter your space. Leave graciously, but always with a smile. It has been said that the eyes are the window of the soul. Don't be a Peeping Tom, but at the same time, keep your windows open and inviting.

In mime, your motions must speak the words you cannot. Exaggeration and emphasis of the essentials of any action are of prime importance. Do not muddy your mime by adding unnecessary actions. You must relearn walking, running and all the actions we take so much for granted. Mime is an art. It is a stylized form that takes practice and imagination. Mime also helps your ability to communicate, by understanding your own body and how it moves, and in understanding the body language of others. Our bodies often scream what our mouths can in no way verbalize.

These notes, of course, are very basic, but they cover just about all the information you need to share with the participants in this initial workshop. Additional workshops can be scheduled for your clown troupe at a later date which focus entirely on mime. There are a number of basic exercises which we find useful as introductions to mime. Additional exercises are provided and can be used as time permits.

BEGINNING EXERCISES

The Wall

Create an imaginary wall and explore its limits. See how convincing you can be. You might want to continue the exercise with the discovery and opening of a window, a door, etc.

Mirroring I

Pair up the participants and have them face each other, standing. Let them touch hands (flat). Have one of the pair start as leader and the other follow every movement of the leader without talking or directing. This exercise should last about three minutes. Switch roles and repeat the procedure. There should be no talking throughout this exercise.

Mirroring II

Again, get your participants into pairs. In this exercise, one person will be a bathroom mirror. The other will go through the usual morning routine — brushing teeth, combing hair, washing face and hands, putting on make-up, etc. Remind the mirrors that they only reflect and never initiate. After about three minutes, switch roles and repeat.

ADDITIONAL MIME EXERCISES

Give each person a chance to perform an exercise. We suggest that you prepare slips of paper with mime exercises written on them in advance so you need only distribute when needed. The participants will need time to think up a routine. They should be encouraged to be as creative as possible in the time given them. Begin with mime exercises for individuals, and as the participants loosen up, move on into pairs and groups.

Here are some examples of mime exercises for you to use. The list will be as large as your imagination allows.

Mime Exercises for Individuals

Hand Mimes

- Paste a stamp to a letter. (Have the stamp stick to your hand.)

- Open and close a door (perhaps one from which you were told to stay away).
- Clean a window.
- Balance a stick on your palm.
- Work a toy top.
- Replace a light bulb.
- Wrap a package.
- Paint a picture.
- Smell a flower.
- Slice a cake and eat a piece.
- Fly a kite.
- Play a trombone.
- Feed the birds.
- Polish your shoes (maybe with them on?).
- Adjust a TV picture.
- Adjust a wall hanging (painting, window shade, drape, etc.).

Look Who I Am

- firefighter
- dressmaker
- trucker
- jeweler
- teacher
- waiter
- plumber
- farmer
- postal clerk
- florist
- surveyor
- bus driver
- astronaut
- nurse
- surgeon
- gardener

Look, Ma, I'm a Sport

- golf
- soccer
- tennis
- croquet
- water skiing
- bowling
- archery
- hurdle-jumping
- ping pong
- weight lifting
- darts
- ice hockey
- throwing a discus
- volleyball
- high jump

Where Am I?

- in a submarine
- in a zoo
- in a cafeteria
- on a picnic
- in a canoe
- in the hospital
- in a closet
- at the museum
- on a roof
- on a train
- in a library
- in a spacecraft
- in a taxi
- in a tree
- at the firehouse

You're an Animal

- giraffe
- dog
- eagle
- turtle

- frog
- unicorn
- sheep
- cat
- camel
- deer

- fox
- bull
- whale
- swan
- bee

Mime Exercise for Pairs

Working Together

- carpenter and helper
- magician and assistant
- priest and acolyte
- Jack and the giant
- boy getting his first haircut
- doctor and patient
- cowboy and wild horse
- bank teller and customer
- boss and secretary
- director and student actor
- grocery clerk and customer
- two runners in a race
- parent teaching child to cook
- an animal trainer and a lion
- lost pedestrian asking for directions
- a person walking his/her dog

Mime Exercises for Groups

Parables

The Gospels can be a rich source of miming exercises, so ask a group of participants to mime a parable. The parable can be read by one of the group as the other clowns act out the story.

Parade

Create a circus parade in mime. Encourage everyone to do his/her thing as singles or in pairs. Everyone is to do a mime as if he/she were part of the circus parade. Suggest some of the following:

- March in step.

- High-step.

- left (or right) foot only

- Clap a rhythm (try to step to every other beat).

- Alternate people turning right and left, then come together again in the other direction.

- Salute and hold.

- March in double time.

- March in swing time.

- Step and stand like statues in position.

Chapter VIII:

THE MINISTRY OF THE CLOWN

There are a number of resource works which help us define the elements of the clown minister. Two works specifically are cited for their relevance to this workshop. The first is *The Clown As Minister*, by Janet Litherland, [1] in which the author categorizes the clown minster as an entertainer, a mediator and a healer.

Tim Kehl sees the clown as a symbol of joy, a symbol of hope, the clown as a nonconformist and the clown as a vulnerable lover in *Getting Started in Clown Ministry*. [2]

There are other sources that you, as facilitator, may be interested in exploring while you prepare for your workshop. The resources are listed in Chapter XIII.

> **66** *The clown can be effective even if he is not accomplished. His own vulnerability enables him to understand the needs of his audience and enables the audience to identify with him. He can at one time minister to all ages, all intellects, all strata of society, the living and the dying. His appearance affects the world without logic, without restrictions — a world where problems and burdens are exchanged for freedom and enlightenment. It is in this world that the clown and his audience move slowly toward each other until they overlap. Ministry takes place at the point of overlapping.* **99** [3]

Fool, buffoon, jester, clown. We've been using these words throughout the workshop, and we've spent some time trying to define our own concepts of what a clown is.

Our workshop is not simply called "A Clown Workshop." This title denotes the learning of skills to become a secular clown. The word *ministry* is in our title to denote one very important difference between secular clowning and Christian clowning. This word, *ministry*, is important because

[1] Litherland, Janet, *The Clown as Minister* (Colorado Springs, Colorado: Meriwether Publishing Ltd., Contemporary Drama Service, 1981).

[2] Kehl, Tim, "Getting Started in Clown Ministry" (Nashville: Clown Ministry Cooperative). Used by permission.

[3] Litherland, *The Clown as Minister*.

it derives from a Latin word meaning *servant,* and the clown minister is, above all else, a servant. In fact, the clown minister exists only to serve; to put aside individual personal needs and feelings to become, for a brief moment, a servant *of* Christ, *for* Christ, and *with* Christ.

Servanthood is not a radical or new concept. Jesus made us all servants. And He gave us the example He wished us to follow on the night before He died.

Jesus took some time out of His schedule to celebrate a religious festival with His friends that night. And after they had shared bread and wine, Jesus knelt before each of His friends and washed the dust off his feet. You have to remember that this foot-washing, while a standard courtesy in the Near East even today, was usually performed by the lowest servants in the household — usually the slaves.

And Jesus said to His friends after He finished His task that, while He is Lord and Master, He, too, must perform this lowliest of tasks. *"You are to do as I have done for you,"* He tells them. (John 13:15)

The focus of a Christian clown, then, is the Servant of Servants and the King of Kings. Jesus is our exemplar. He is the great clown. No disrespect or derision is meant in this statement. The clown is the ultimate servant. His name comes from *clod* (a clump of earth), the most common of the common, the serf of all. Jesus says, *"He who would be great among you must be servant, and the greatest is he who is everyone's slave."* (Mark 10:43)

If we are to follow Christ's example to serve and to be served, our ministry becomes something more than dressing funny and putting on exaggerated make-up. We need to discover some of the aspects of the clown minister's personality that will help us further define our own clown character.

Christian clowning is especially rewarding for us because it helps us to realize our relationship with Jesus and puts us in touch with the very essentials by which we should all live our Christian lives.

Let's look a little deeper into the list we began this morning. Look at these words: *entertain, teach, love, hope, nonconformity, childlike, healer.* (These words, or words very similar in meaning, have almost always appeared on the lists generated at each of our workshops during the exercise "A Clown is . . ." in Chapter IV.) We were using these words to characterize our idea of what a clown is. But don't they also represent some of the essential things that Christ asks us to be? Perhaps we can find the *essence* of the clown minister's personality in some of these words.

JOY

66 *I am willing to act like a fool in order to show my joy in the Lord.* **99** (2 Samuel 6:21)

King David makes this remark to his daughter in a very jubilant account of the return of the Ark of the Covenant to Jerusalem. It says something about our relationship with God, doesn't it? The clown reminds us of how joyful we can be. *"The clown is a joyful player who celebrates life, glories in simple things and delights in children."* [4]

Becoming a clown minister is a joy — joy in the context of prayer, study and service — the tripod of Christian life and renewal. Only one who feels true joy can bring true joy. Consider the joy of Mary Magdalene when Jesus showed her freedom and true joy. As a clown minister, you, too, can be Jesus's agent of joy.

HEALER

The clown can be a healer, if only for a fleeting moment, because the clown carries the cross a step or two. The clown is called to take the role of Simon of Cyrene. *"He shows us the best cure for inner pain — loving action — and through his own pain, he is able to heal."* [5]

The clown puts on his/her whiteface, wipes out his/her ego, and his/her personal traits disappear. He/she puts on the death mask of the whiteface clown, and then seeks the features which God inspires him/her to accept — perhaps a set of bright eyes exposing the soul of the clown; perhaps a tear which says, "I'll cry for you — let me have your sadness;" or a smile that says, "Forget your cares, your concerns, and let's play together — smile my smile, take my joy." The clown is a fool who stumbles over his/her shadow, hammers his/her thumb, and plays with moonbeams.

And yet, the clown is also the exaggerated foolishness of every time you have been embarrassed, every time you felt like the idiot in this sophisticated world. He/she is there to say, "You think it was strange coming to church in your jeans when everyone else was dressed up? Look at me in my floppy shoes and baggy pants.

[4] Kehl, "Getting Started in Clown Ministry."

[5] Litherland, *The Clown as Minister.*

"Were you embarrassed when you dripped gravy on your new shirt? What about the whipped cream dripping from my face after I just got hit with that pie? Let me direct your attention; let me carry your burden; let me bring you peace and joy and healing, even if it's only for a moment."

ENTERTAINER/TEACHER

We don't know whether we can call Jesus an entertainer or not. He certainly was a good storyteller, and we think this points up something about the clown minister. Yes, the clown entertains, but like Jesus, there must be something more. Through the parables, Jesus was able to teach as well as entertain His friends and the people who came to listen to Him.

But, you say, how can the clown *teach* while simply handing out balloons, or picking imaginary daisies or doing pratfalls?

The clown is the parable of God's salvation, the silent one who shouts God's steadfast love. The clown says, "I am lower than anyone. I am your servant. No matter who you are, I serve *you!*"

66 *Through comedy, the audience is put in touch with a basic truth, and each member of the audience will laugh for his own reasons.* 99 [6]

HOPE

Hope is a very strong force in our lives. We only have to go to the movies to see this clearly. When we go to the movies, our hope is that the hero and/or heroine will be successful when the final frame fades out. We hope for success; we hope to be loved and to love.

Well, the clown minister is a symbol of that hope. There is a little of Abraham in the clown minister. Paul tells us that Abraham's *"faith did not leave him and he did not doubt God's promise; his faith filled him with power and he gave praise to God. He was absolutely sure that God would be able to do what He had promised."* (Romans 4:20-21)

We see the clown attempt to do something. And we know before he/she begins that it will fail. And over and over again, the clown just doesn't seem to be able to get it together. Well, you know, if our movie

[6] Litherland, *The Clown as Minister.*

ended here, we would be very disappointed, wouldn't we? We hope the clown will succeed because he/she has tried so hard. And the clown minister ultimately *does* succeed! This says an awful lot to the person who is confined to a hospital bed, or left to die in a nursing home.

Our Christian lives are sometimes filled with these same kinds of obstacles. We are often frustrated and unable to respond to the demands placed upon us when we try to defend our faith. But we do defend it as we model our lives on Jesus. We can think of His last days on earth and remember His betrayal, arrest, trial and crucifixion, and know that the clown minister can convey hope because of Christ's ultimate victory over darkness.

66 *The resurrection of Jesus is the supreme example of God's refusal to accept the limits of the possible. On Easter, the victim became the victor . . .* 99 [7]

NONCONFORMITY

The clown minister has, throughout history, challenged conventional ways of thinking. There is a phrase that puts it very well. It says that there are two kinds of people who refuse to conform to the limits of the possible: madmen and clowns. Both may wind up behind bars, in straight jackets or on crosses.

Jesus was a nonconformist. He ate with tax collectors and ministered to the sick and the poor.

66 *Like the jester, Christ defies custom and scorns crowned heads. Like a wandering troubadour, He has no place to lay His head. Like the clown in the circus parade, He satirizes existing authority by riding into town replete with regal pageantry when He has no earthly power. Like a minstrel, He frequents dinners and parties. At the end, He is costumed by His enemies in a mocking caricature of royal paraphernalia. He is crucified, amidst sniggers and taunts, with a sign over His head that lampoons His laughable claim.* 99 [8]

We are aware of the outward nonconformity of clowns by the way they dress and the facial features they emphasize. There is no telling what other nonconformities are hidden within the depths of their imaginations, or what other nonconformities transform them into fools for Christ.

[7] Kehl, "Getting Started in Clown Ministry."

[8] Cox, Harvey, *The Feast of Fools* (Cambridge, Mass.: Harvard University Press, 1969). Reprinted by permission.

LOVE

The clown minister loves his/her brothers and sisters as Christ loves us. It never enters the mind of the clown that anyone would want to do him/her harm, and this makes the clown minister vulnerable.

Paul sums up the qualities of love in his first letter to the Corinthians. He writes:

> 66 *Love is patient; love is kind and envies no one. Love is never boastful, nor conceited, nor rude; never selfish, not quick to take offense. Love keeps no score of wrongs; does not gloat over other men's sins, but delights in the truth. There is nothing that love cannot face; there is no limit to its faith, its hope, and its endurance.* 99 (1 Corinthians 13:4-7)

This kind of love takes effort, selflessness and prayers. We are called as clown ministers to all of this. Jesus is the greatest lover.

> 66 *He believes in an inherent goodness in all people and even excused His executioners by saying, ' They know not what they do.'* 99 [9]

MEDIATION

As a teacher, the clown minister can become the mediator between God and human frailties by transforming these frailties into joy.

There is a difference from our usual understanding of this word *mediation* that's important to clown ministry. The clown minister participates in the mediation. We don't usually see an umpire or a referee playing the sport for which they are mediators. But the clown minister will not ask other people to step through the looking glass until he/she has gone through first.

The clown minister says that the most powerful person in the world is the one who gives away his power. Jesus humbled Himself. He came into the world in a lowly stable instead of a royal palace; lived a peasant's life with His eartly parents; and probably pursued the carpentry trade with

[9] Kehl, "Getting Started in Clown Ministry."

Joseph until He became an itinerant preacher, living from handout to handout. St. Paul tells us that, indeed, Jesus humbled Himself, and in total obedience, accepted everything His Father asked of Him, even death upon the cross. (Philippians 2:6-8)

And here, too, the clown minister must follow Jesus' example. The clown minister gives away his/her power, and respects other people's space, never trying to enter into it until he/she is invited. *"It is only as he gives of himself, honestly and spontaneously, that the grace of God is communicated to others."* [10]

CHILDLIKE

We spoke earlier about how Jesus loved children. He tells us that we must accept the kingdom of God as a child. (Mark 10:15) For the clown minister, this means that he/she must become a little less questioning and have a little more faith. The clown must love, trust, play, imagine and create as a child would.

This poem tells us something about a child's world. It is written by a high-school student, Alyce Spencer, from Topeka, Kansas:

In my frustrated world
Of unanswerable algebraic quotations
And notebooks full
of overdue assignments,
My ego declines.

"God, show me simplicity!"
In walks my young brother,
Grinning, impishly.
I think, "No, NO! I wanted simplicity.
I got my young brother."

But as I sit there thinking
Of what punishment I might receive
From Mrs. Attlebury for not doing my math,
My young brother calls out to me.
He appeals, "Watch this!"
Slowly, but surely, he ties his shoe
And looks to me for a sign of approval.
I smile, and notice.

[10] Litherland, *The Clown as Minister.*

Simplicity did walk in the door,
I began to reason more and more.
And I realize that
A sky of yellow and clouds of orange
Survive only in a world
Seen through a child's eyes.
Pain is but a scratch
And sorrow is knowing today can't last.
Happiness is playing with one's best friend,
And education comes through daydreaming.
For that, I grin ear to ear.

I guess we're all just grown-up children
Falling dangerously into the busy world.
We're all schemers.
But we're losing our childlike visions.
We just can't seem to hold on to them.

As I return to my math book,
Staring at me blankly, I know,
If we need simplicity in our days,
We can watch a young child at play. [11]

There's a warning about being childlike, and the clown minister must recognize the tendency. St. Paul says in his first letter to the Corinthians: *"Do not be childish, my friends. Be as innocent of evil as babes, but at least be grown-up in your thinking."* (1 Corinthians 14:20)

The clown minister creates an environment where people can experience the joy and love of God. Creating that environment makes the clown childlike. Working at our ministry as though a child helps us to open ourselves to respond with loving action. We *are* nonconformists, and we *become* vulnerable because we are childlike and loving.

So the clown minister symbolizes many things, and we can see parallels in the life of Jesus that help us in creating our own clown character.

And when we lose sight of our purpose, we can reread Paul's advice to the Corinthians:

66 *For consider your call, brethren. Not many of you were wise according to worldly standards, not many were powerful, not many were of noble birth; but God chose what is foolish in the world to shame the wise; God chose what is weak in the world to shame the strong; God chose what*

[11] *Spencer, Alyce, untitled poem first appearing in POWER Magazine (summer, 1982). Published by Christian Youth Publications, St. Charles, Mo.*

is low and despised in the world; even things that are not, to bring to nothing things that are; so that no human being might boast in the presence of God. (1 Corinthians 1:2)

We belong to a society that places enormous emphasis on upward mobility and material success. All this emphasis and psychological patterning supplies strokes to the successful and blows to those who do not fit the guidelines. Jesus' ministry says success in the world is an illusion; ministry to the beautiful people only is without heavenly reward. Accumulating treasure on earth invites the anxiety of protection.

Jesus also says, *"As you do for one of these least of My children, you do for Me."* The fool for Christ says, "I am the minister to the unlovely; I go where angels fear and others dare not. I go through the gates of death for you."

If you choose to be a clown, you choose abandonment of the world's norms, and the world's ideals and goals. As a clown, it is Christ that shines through. Not in big letters or brassy patter, but in love, concern and compassion.

In this light, the clown must be strengthened by prayer and supported by all that the local church can do, for the clown is a minister, an outreach, an extension of your church family to a broken and pain-filled world. This is not a ministry to be undertaken lightly, but with solemn levity and a vow to bring the joy and peace of the Lord to those in need, even though it might only be a momentary, fleeting experience.

The only one who brings peace beyond understanding and joy without end is Jesus Himself, and in that, we can only point the way and say, "He is here, follow Him!"

Chapter IX:

TOOLS OF THE CLOWN

There are a number of elements or tools that the clown can call upon to realize his/her character.

While the areas of mime, props, costume and make-up seem a little obvious, there are some points for which a special emphasis will help the participants reinforce their concept of clown ministry.

MIME

We've already said that a clown troupe does not have to elect a silent ministry. But if you have chosen it, then pantomime is an important element.

We've been doing some mime exercises today, and we should realize now that how we move our bodies and use our eyes is very important. If you keep in mind that mime really does not communicate words, but rather expresses emotions and thoughts, body movement and eye contact become of even greater importance.

"Silence is golden," we're told. If this is so, the silent clown is a powerful minister. The actions of the clown can convince an audience to suspend disbelief for a few moments.

(If time permits, you might want to do a quick mime exercise here for reinforcement.)

PROPS

A prop is anything that is essential to the action or to the character that does not fall under the category of costume or make-up: balloons, pompons, an oversized cigar, imaginary dog on a leash, etc.

(If balloons, such as "apple" or "bee" balloons, are used which require instruction for assembly, take time here to instruct participants. You might want to have a "bag of tricks" available containing kazoos, artificial flowers, funny hats, etc.)

COSTUME

Let's face it: we dress the way we dress, most of the time, because our friends and this society we live in place limitations upon us. They tell us how to dress for school, for church, for the job interview. We're told what we must wear when we jog, when we ski, go dancing or sun ourselves at the beach.

We said that the clown is a nonconformist. And when we get rid of the limitations of dress codes, we can begin to do outlandish things. The costume helps you to become a new person. It can be as elaborate or as simple as your clown character demands. The concept will not become apparent all at once, but will develop as your clown character grows.

(Ask participants to share their costume ideas with the group. Ask if the idea has changed since the session began this morning. What have you brought with you? You can share your own costume ideas at this time and how the character has evolved.)

MAKE-UP

We also create a new person when we put on make-up. We enter into this servant role we have chosen only when we wipe out our petty peeves and irritabilities and selfishnesses. We apply clown white to our faces and create a death mask, and as we do so, we symbolically die to self.

Our Lord made it plain that true discipleship was not a matter of being blessed with things, but of dying to self. Without such dying, our prayer life and our life as servants are hopelessly empty. We can ask ourselves what exactly *dying to self* means. An unknown writer answered this question with these six thoughts:

66 *When you are forgotten or neglected or purposely set at naught, and you don't sting and hurt with the insult or the oversight, but your heart is happy, being counted worthy to suffer for Christ,* that is dying to self.

66 *When your good is evil spoken of, when your wishes are crossed, your advice disregarded, your opinions ridiculed, and you refuse to let anger rise in your heart, or even defend yourself, but take it all in patient, loving silence,* that is dying to self.

66 *When you are content with any food, any rainment, any climate, any society, any solitude, any interruption by the will of God,* that is dying to self.

66 *When you never care to refer to yourself in conversation, or record your own good works, or itch after commendation, when you truly love to be unknown,* that is dying to self.

66 *When you can see your brother prosper and have his needs met, and can honestly rejoice with him in spirit and feel no envy nor question God, though your own needs are far greater and you are in desperate circumstances,* that is dying to self.

66 *When you can receive correction and reproof from someone of less stature than yourself, and can humbly submit inwardly as well as outwardly, finding no resentment or rebellion rising up in your heart,* that is dying to self. 99 [1]

Our old self slowly disappears as we cover up the many things we don't like about ourselves. When our face is completely whitened, there is nothing left of the old self — no eyebrows, eyelashes, mustaches, wrinkles or lines, zits, birthmarks — we've covered up everything. We have "killed" ourselves, in a way. Fortunately, this death is reversible.

And this is part of the tradition of the clown. When the clown applies the whiteface, no further harm can come to him/her. With this symbolic

[1] "Dying to Self," author unknown

death comes freedom — freedom to become vulnerable, loving and non-conforming. Do you suppose Jesus had the clown in mind when He said, *"He who finds life will lose it, and he who loses his life for My sake will find it."* ? (Matthew 10:38)

You see, the clown character laughs at death! There was a time in history when bad news was related to the king through the jester because bearers of bad news were usually beheaded, and, since the jester was already dead, he could not be killed again.

The colors and the markings that we apply over the clown white become symbols of *new life.* We add back some of the characteristics that we like about ourselves (the good things are wiped away also when we put on the clown white). We add the good things, but we do so with a difference. We accent our eyes, show off our mouths, add vibrant colors to show our happiness and nonconformity; in a sense, we are reborn, just as Christ was reborn on that first Easter morning.

We now know a little more about our ministry as "fools for Christ," and we have learned about costume and make-up and how these tools help us create our clown character.

So what *is* a clown? Is he/she hiding behind a mask? Is he/she ignoring all his/her bad aspects and pretending to be someone other than who he/she really is? Is this just another cop-out?

(Take a few minutes to discuss.)

Of course, none of these things is so:

66 *When a clown becomes a clown, he makes a free gift of himself to his audience. To endow them with the saving grace of laughter, he submits himself to being mocked, drenched, clouted, crossed in love.* **99** [2]

This personal willingness to give up static and preconceived notions of how God's people are served makes the clown a seeker more than a hider; a mover, not a cop-out; in fact, it makes the clown a *minister of God!*

[2] West, Morris, *The Clowns of God*
    (New York: William Morrow & Co., Inc.)

Chapter X

OUT OF DEATH, NEW LIFE

This is the second faith imagination exercise. It is used just prior to applying make-up. We cannot emphasize strongly enough the need to familiarize yourselves with this type of exercise before you attempt to use it. (Refer to introductory comments concerning faith imagination exercises in Chapter IV.)

Relaxation Exercise

Here, the nature of your group will determine how you proceed. Have participants lie on the floor once again. You may wish to repeat the whole relaxation exercise as described in Chapter V, or simply start with them sinking into a cloud. How you start will depend on the amount of tension that seems evident.

A Meditation on Whiteface

(This is not to be read. It is only put in print for use as a sample from which to draw ideas and direction. We use background music, a simple piano solo of "Send in the Clowns," throughout the exercise and into the section on make-up. The exercise should take between five and seven minutes.)

Sample monolog:

We are being invited once again to enter into the world of imagination — to let go and listen only to my voice. Close your eyes. Let go and listen. See yourself. See yourself sitting in front of a mirror. Look at yourself right through the mirror. See yourself.

Now take some clown white. Put it on. Go ahead. Your forehead, your eyebrows, your eyes — down further and further. Everything disappears — all those distinctive features gone — and all you can see is white.

Now apply that whiteface — that death mask, for that is what it is — apply that whiteface to your ego, too, that me-centeredness, me-serving-ness of your person. Put aside your needs, your desires, your program. Let go, for Jesus invites you to serve Him, to serve Him by serving your brothers and sisters. To serve as a fool, a clown, a helpless, helpless soul. But to do that, you must die. You must kill all of that self-serving part of you. You must become a servant. Servanthood isn't easy and it isn't cheap. It costs everything.

Jesus Himself paid a price much higher than anything it might cost you. He gave up His right to be God. He gave up being in His Father's presence. He gave up the whole royal scene and became a man — a child — helpless and weak. He cried and cooed, and dirtied His diapers. He grew up a Joe, the carpenter's kid. He hung out with Rocky and the gang. He chose the life of an itinerant preacher, accused of heresy and treason. He was beaten, spit upon, humiliated and executed in one of the most barbaric procedures devised by man.

This is the King — this is He who said, *"I have given you an example; go and do likewise."* Under His humanity was hidden His majesty — the Servant King.

Your time has come, for He who dies that you may live kneels before you now. See Him, splendid and yet pathetic. See Him take up His towel and basin. He washes your feet. Look into His eyes. See there the love. Be warmed in that love. Be fulfilled in that love. See the wounds in His hands and know His love, and hear Him.

Hear Him as He says, *"You call Me master and Lord, and so I am. If I, your Lord, have washed your feet, can you do less for these, My little ones? that child confined to a hospital room? that downtrodden person in the wrong part of town? that forgotten elder in the nursing home? Feed My lambs. I will strengthen you. I will sustain you.*

"Put on the masks of death, and just as My life did not end in My ultimate death, so your mask is now complete in its whiteness, but you accent it with color — colors of life — born anew as a servant, born to serve My lambs. To take on their pain, their sorrow, their loneliness — even if only for a moment. Help them. Free them. Free them. Let them have your life."

For the next moment in silence except for the music, let Jesus minister to you, so you can go minister to His friends. *(Leave at least a minute's silence before you start to bring participants back. Slowly have them return. Tell them to sit up when they are ready.)*

Instruction will begin in techniques of applying make-up.

Chapter XI:

PUTTING IT INTO PRACTICE

A reasonable amount of time needs to be allotted for the application of make-up. A novice will require more time than a "pro." For most of the participants, this first application of clown white will be a smelly, greasy, messy business, and it takes a little pushing of oneself to put that first bit of "glop" (clown white) on one's face.

Participants should have been instructed to come prepared with mirrors and materials that might be used as a clown costume. If any article of clothing is to be put on over the head, the participant should costume *before* applying the clown white.

Tables and chairs should have been set up in advance so that no time is lost between the meditation and the making-up. If space permits, set-up can be accomplished during the lunch break.

The arrangement of tables should be a "U" shape, with the table at the "bottom" of the "U" set up for those facilitators who will be applying make-up. Enough space should be provided at the tables to avoid crowding. It is difficult to apply the make-up if you're rubbing elbows with the person next to you.

We ask that everyone take the make-up applicaton step by step and follow the facilitator. We ask this of everyone, regardless of how many times they have made-up. Obviously, the people who have applied make-up before should help those who have not (a wonderful first step toward the servant ministry of the clown minister).

Since our focus is on the ministry of the clown as exemplified by Jesus' servant ministry, and as we are to begin "dying to self" by applying clown white, we begin the making-up process by asking for God's guidance and protection.

We have found one of the following prayers always suitable at this time:

THE CLOWN'S PRAYER

66 *Dear Lord, help me create more laughter than tears, disperse more happiness than gloom, spread more cheer than despair. Never let me grow so big that I fail to see the wonder in the eyes of a child or the twinkle in the eyes of the aged. Never let me forget that I am a clown . . . that my work is to cheer people up, make them happy, and allow them to laugh; to forget momentarily all the unpleasant things in their lives. Never let me forget to call upon my Creator in my hour of need or acknowledge Him in my hours of plenty. Amen.* **99** [1]

PRAYER OF SELF-DEDICATION

66 *Almighty and eternal God, so draw our hearts to Thee, so guide our minds, so fill our imaginations, so control our wills, that we may be wholly Thine, utterly dedicated unto Thee; and then use us, we pray Thee, as Thou wilt, and always to Thy glory and for the welfare of Thy people; through our Lord and Savior Jesus Christ. Amen.* **99** [2]

You may feel more comfortable with extemporaneous prayer(s), from either participant(s) or facilitator(s).

The exercise below is also effective as you begin the making-up process.

Look in My Window — See My Daddy
---

[1] Meyer, Charles R., *How to Be a Clown* (David McKay Co.).

[2] From the *Book of Common Prayer* of the Episcopal Church in the United States.

Pair the participants up and have them stand facing each other, fingertip to fingertip. Those in each pair are to look into each other's eyes. This may be difficult at first. Expect some giggling, especially if the pairs are really friendly with each other. Continue to maintain eye contact for one minute.

After resting for a moment, have the pairs resume their positions fingertip to fingertip, and while looking into each other's eyes, they recite the Lord's Prayer.

Next, have each person repeat the Lord's Prayer (first one, then the other) in a personal form: something akin to . . . "John, your Daddy and mine, who is in heaven, is holy. I pray that His kingdom and His will are right here with us . . ."

To set the proper mood and to focus on our silent ministry, participants should be told that after the moment that clown white is first applied, they continue to make-up in silence, speaking only when necessary to ask for assistance. The spirit of the earlier meditation can be maintained by utilizing the music tape throughout the make-up period.

If time permits, go through a few mime exercises after make-up and costuming are completed.

Take pictures of each participant (using instant-developing film) which will be attached to the "graduation" diplomas at the end of the workshop.

THE MAKING-UP PROCESS

1. The first thing we do is apply clown white to all exposed areas of the face, ears and neck. Take a small amount of the clown white and put it in the palm of your hand and work it with the fingers. This procedure makes the clown white more pliable as it warms up and softens, and easier to apply to the face. Don't take too much. You'll see that a little goes a long way, and it's easier to take some more from the jar than to get rid of excess on the palm of your hand. Spread the clown white evenly over the entire facial area. To get it smooth, pat the face with the tips of the fingers. Don't forget the neck and the ears.

Clowns who do not paint the neck are called "dirty-neck clowns" because of the difference in color between the whiteface and the natural skin tone.

Do not go on to the next step until everyone has applied the clown white. Take a moment to reflect on the "death mask" that everyone has applied. Ask each participant to study his/her features (or lack of features) in the mirror as you re-emphasize "death to self."

2. **We begin to build the new person by first removing the clown white in areas that will be covered with color.** This is done with cotton swabs, tissues, etc. It is essential that all the areas where color is to be used are cleansed of clown white, as colors will run and/or become milky and dull if applied over clown white.

    Again, everyone does this together, and we do not go on until everyone can continue. Help each other as much as possible.

3. **When everyone has eliminated clown white in the areas where color is to be applied,** *everyone* **powders.** White talcum powder is placed in a heavy white sock, which is used as the "puff." The entire made-up area is powdered — the more, the better, as powdering helps "set" or dry the clown white. The powder is patted on, rather than rubbed. Excess powder is then removed with a very soft brush (a baby's hair brush is ideal). Be careful not to brush off the clown white.

4. **After everyone has brushed and powdered, colors are added** *one by one.* Each time a color is added to the face, the clown must powder and brush, taking extra care now so that colors will not run into the white. Remember, you add colors *one by one* — first the black, then the red.

    We have always limited our clowns at this initial workshop to the use of red and black, simply because time doesn't permit the application of additional colors. You may tell the participants that they can add more colors the next time they make-up. Point out that yellow grease paint has a chemical in the yellow dye that is an irritant to the eyes, so yellow should not be applied around the eyes.

    [During the time when people are applying clown white, you might want to read "Clowns Put a New Face on Celebration of Mass," an article by Laura Durkin (see appendix).]

5. **When the complete clown is made-up, and the face is powdered for the last time, the entire made-up area is squirted with a mist of water** (old, sterile spray bottles from cleaning products such as Windex or Glass Plus are useful). Have paper towels handy so that the excess water which will drip from the face can be patted off. *Do not wipe water off the make-up,* as the misting completes the setting or drying process. As the water

dries, you will feel the make-up get stiff and harden. Even though you are "set," you must take care of your make-up. Be careful when you put on the rest of your costume, and suppress the urge to scratch your nose. You can still smudge your make-up.

If time permits, you might like to try other pantomime exercises, or allow the participants to think up routines they can use during the practical experience they are about to receive.

The time has come to take your neophyte clown ministers into the world. Walk or drive to the facility where you have made arrangements, or go to a nearby park or playground, and be servants for Christ.

Expect a bit of shyness and groupiness at first, but if all goes as our experience indicates, the thrill of ministry will break down these early barriers.

Instruct your ministers that, as they have become a different person, one that is now bigger than life, no one should be seen doing something ordinary like chewing gum, eating, smoking etc.

And remember, *silence*!

We have found it advisable to have at least one person who does not make-up to act as spokesperson for the group during the ministry time. It helps to explain to the frightened why these clowns cannot talk to them.

Chapter XII

GO, THEN, IN CHRIST'S NAME AND BRING JOY

Try to maintain the silence as much as possible as you return to the workshop facility; the younger the group, the more difficult this will be.

Gather as a community. While still in whiteface, you will break the silence just long enough for the participants to share some of what the experience has meant to them, or perhaps to share some special part of their initial ministerial experience. Don't drag this "critique" out. In brevity, there is power!

The final moments of the workshop are about to begin. The nature of this portion will depend greatly on the communion from which you come. We will describe the service as we have done it in the Episcopal Diocese of Long Island.

Assemble the group around the altar (in the church or a portable altar set up in the workshop facility). The only persons *not* in whiteface are the priest or minister and the group spokesperson. Silence has been reimposed on the community, and all responses during the worship service are *mimed*.

We used Eucharistic Rite II from the *Book of Common Prayer* of the Episcopal Church in the United States. Collect is either the collect for ministry (page 256) or the prayer for new ministry (pages 562 and 563). Only one reading is used, since the exhausting nature of the day precludes use of any more than one.

We suggest one of the following:

- John 13:1-17
- John 15:12-20
- Matthew 23:1-12
- Matthew 18:1-5
- Mark 9:33-37

Prayers of the People can either be a form with silent responses or a free form with the possibility of a nonverbal response. We usually omit the Confession of Sin and the Creed. The important part of the *pro-anafera* is the Peace.

We indicate that the Peace represents renewal and the redemption to the community. We have the participants again form pairs to remove each other's make-up as a sign of the community's full acceptance of this person made new. This will take some time, as the participants will want to remove all the make-up they can at once.

Instructions for removing make-up are relatively simple. A generous amount of cold cream or vegetable shortening (cheaper than cold cream, but equally as effective) is warmed first in the hands and then gently rubbed all over the made-up areas. The resultant gray "goop" is then wiped off with paper towels. Several applications may be required to remove all the make-up. Encourage gentleness. The majority of make-up will be removed this way. Some color residue may remain, but this will wash off with soap and water.

Continue the celebration after everyone has had a chance to remove the majority of his/her make-up. Consecration, the Lord's Prayer, and Communion follow. Diplomas are handed out immediately following the Eucharist.

After the prayer of thanksgiving and a closing song (perhaps "They Will Know We Are Christians by Our Love"), dismiss the community with these words: "Go into the world as Christ's fools and bring joy to all His children." The response is, "Thanks be to God!"

Any last-minute cleaning up of the facility and of participants' faces should be done, and participants sent off as quickly as possible. Note that rapid cleansing helps prevent any possibly serious facial infections.

It is important that you not let clown ministry drop here. Plan several future dates when your troupe will be able to minister.

Enjoy your workshop and pray for us in our ministry. God bless you.

Chapter XIII:

RESOURCES

We believe that the resource listing on this and the following pages represents one of the most complete annotated listings dealing with the subject of clowning.

We have assembled a cross section of materials that have been helpful in our own research as well as those which are resources for locating hard-to-find items of apparel, instructional materials and institutions, and audio and visual aids.

Part of this listing was developed by Mary Jo Parnell from Memphis, Tennessee, and given to us for use in our workshop. Mary Jo and her troupe have been active in liturgical clowning and street mime in Memphis for several years.

We solicit any information or resources that might be useful in expanding this listing in future editions. Your comments on these or any other resources in this area would also be helpful.

AUDIO CASSETTES

The Complete Floyd Shaffer Clown Ministry Workshop Kit. Six cassettes by clown minister Floyd Shaffer. A complete training package covering: 1. Biblical foundation of clown ministry; 2. history of the clown; 3. getting in touch; 4. imagination growth; 5. plunge into the world; 6. clues on make-up; and 7. party session and more. Available through Contemporary Drama Service, P.O. Box 7710, Colorado Springs, CO 80933, (303) 594-4422. Kit of six cassettes in vinyl binder.

CIRCUS

Burgess, Hovey. *Circus Techniques.* Drama Specialists. New York, 1977.

Kirk, Rhina. *Circus Heroes and Heroines.* Hammond, Wisconsin, 1972.

CIRCUS MUSIC

AMERICAN INTERNATIONAL GALLERIES, INC., Irvine, CA 92714. "The Taj Mahal in Concert." 33⅓ rpm recording, stereo. Recorded by Corky Griffin. A very famous theatre organ with some tunes you will find helpful in clown ministry.

CULTURAL HERITAGE AND ARTS CENTER, P.O. Box 1275, 1000 Second, Dodge City, KS 67801. Has two albums available:

"Big Top: Circus Calliope." Stereo disc AFSD 5986. Featuring the Wurlitzer Calliola at Paul Eakin's Gay 90s Village, Silkeston, MO.

"Circus Carnival: Calliope." Stereo disc AFSD 5958.

TAGGERT ENTERPRISES, 1602 National Ave., Rockford, IL 61103. Calliope, stereo 33⅓ rpm album. Old-time circus music played by Barb Taggert.

CLOWN MINISTRY

Adams, Doug. *Humor in the American Pulpit.* Austin: The Sharing Company. Pioneer work of scholarship in assessing the significance of humor theologically and historically in American preaching. On the surface, this volume has nothing to do with clowning, but should be helpful for individuals who use their clowning as part of the liturgy. Available through The Sharing Company, P.O. Box 2224, Austin, TX.

Ambrose, Susan Foster. "The Healing Magic of Clowns." *Kiwanis Magazine.* October, 1979. Page 26.

Editor. "Clowning Around." Interview with clown minister Floyd Shaffer, who shares some ideas to guide a group into clown ministry. *GROUP Magazine.* Colorado Springs, CO, December, 1979.

Editors. *The Youth Group How-To Book.* A practical collection of 60 youth group projects and programs that have appeared in *GROUP Magazine* over the years. Includes a section on clown ministry. Group Books, Box 481, Loveland, CO 80539.

Feit, Kenneth. "The Priestly Fool." Anglican Theological Review. Vol. 5, June, 1975.

Kehl, Tim. "Getting Started in Clown Ministry." Part of "Shoddy Pad" communications series, 1978, six pages. Talks about theology of clowning and gives helpful hints on how to start a clown ministry in a local church. There is an illustrated section on clown make-up. Available from the Office of Communication Education (United Methodist), 1525 McGavock St., Nashville, TN 37203, or The Clown Ministry Cooperative, Box 24023, Nashville, TN 37202.

Litherland, Janet. *The Clown Ministry Handbook.* Contemporary Drama Service, P.O. Box 7710, Colorado Springs, CO 80933, (303) 594-4422. The first complete text on the art of clown ministry. An exceptionally helpful book covering history, current activities, make-up, costumes, props and several clown sketches. A complete reference for all basics.

Nicholls, Thomas. "The Praise of Folly." Nicholls is chaplain for the Clowns of America, and his "Praise of Folly" articles appear regularly in *The Calliope,* official magazine of the organization.

Shaffer, Floyd T. "The Clown: Another Fool for Christ's Sake." *Military Chaplains' Review,* 1979. Pages 15-22.

Shaffer, Floyd T. *If I Were a Clown.* Augsburg Publishing House, Minneapolis, MN. More on clowning by a leading clown minister.

Shaffer and Sewall. *Clown Ministry.* Group Books, Box 481, Loveland, CO 80539. A how-to manual with skits.

Stone, David. *The Complete Youth Ministries Handbook.* Creative Models, Shreveport, LA, 1979. This handbook is a compilation of articles promoting a wholistic approach to youth ministry. The article "Just Clownin' Around" is written by Bill Peckham.

CLOWNING — SECULAR

Hartisch, Karl, "Whitey." *Introduction to Clowning.* This book covers all aspects of clowning — make-up, clown characters, costuming, clown gestures, acting, ethics and rules of behavior, and is available through Clowns of America, P.O. Box 30, Eaglesville, PA 19408.

Meyer, Charles R. *How to Be a Clown.* David McKay Co., New York, 1977.

Sanders, Toby. *How to Be a Complete Clown.* Stein and Day, New York, 1978.

Stolzenberg, Mark. *The Clown for Circus and Stage.* Sterling Publishing Co., New York, 1981.

Towsen, John H. *Clowns.* Hawthorn Books Inc., New York, 1976.

Wiley, Jack. *Basic Circus Skills.* Stackpole Books, Harrisburg, PA, 1974.

EQUIPMENT SOURCES

Most clowning supplies are available in your locality from party supply or theatre supply houses. Some specialty items, however, may be difficult to obtain, and are listed here for your convenience.

THE CIRCUS CLOWNS, 2835 Nicollet Ave., Minneapolis, MN 55408. A mail order company that has everything from handmade clown hats to giant buttons. Instruction materials are also available. Write for a catalog.

CONTEMPORARY DRAMA SERVICE, P.O. Box 7710, Colorado Springs, CO 80933, (303) 594-4422. The Ben Nye Klown Kit is designed especially for clowns and mimes. It contains plenty of professional clown white, a black pencil, white face powder, velour powder puff, latex sponge applicators, make-up remover, a custom #3 flat brush and a Rainbow Wheel of six cream make-up colors. An eight-ounce can of Ben Nye's special clown white is available, too. Write for price information.

CLOWN, MIME, PUPPET AND DANCE MINISTRY COOPERATIVE, 1525 McGavock St., Nashville, TN 37203, (615) 327-0911. Handles balloons for balloon sculpture, Mehron and Stein cosmetics. Send for order form/price list. Check or money order must accompany orders. Note: This service just covers a basic number of items: clown white, grease pencils, red and black liner and soft grease paint, and major balloons used in clown balloon sculpture.

CUSTOM COSTUMES BY BETTY, Betty Cash, 2181 Edgerton St., St. Paul, MN 55117, (612) 771-8734. Professionally done clown costumes. Write for styles and price information.

CUSTOM-MADE SHOES, John, the Clown Shoemaker, 2521 W. Berwyn, Chicago, IL 60625, (312) 728-1039. Professional clown shoes in a variety of styles handmade to order by an orthopedic shoemaker.

JUGGLE BUG, 23004 107th Place West, Edmonds, IA 98020. Distributor of supplies for jugglers — books, scarves, balls, rings, clubs and cigar boxes.

RECREATION NOVELTY, 221-23 Park Ave., Baltimore, MD 21101, (301) 727-8397. This company offers sturdy balloons imprinted with the word "Love." Used in clown worship events or for giving away in shopping malls, hospitals . . . wherever your clown group is carrying on its special ministry.

TAL WORLD-WIDE PRODUCTIONS, 717 Beverly Rd., Baltimore, MD 21222, (301) 285-4848. Carries a complete line of juggling equipment.

TIPP NOVELTY COMPANY, 222 North Sixth St., Tipp City, OH 45371, (513) 667-2444. Tipp Novelty is a major supplier of giveaway items . . . almost every conceivable type of trinket and doodad. Catalog describes everything from smile balloons to inexpensive plastic kazoos.

FAITH IMAGINATION

Peal, Dr. Norman Vincent. *Dynamic Imaging.* Guidepost Press, New York, 1980.

Spata, James P. *Faith Imagination and the Clown Workshop.* A tape of faith imagination exercises from this workshop available from Youth Ministries, Episcopal Diocese of Long Island, Garden City, NY 11530.

de Paola, Tomie. *The Clown of God.* Harcourt Brace Jovanovich, New York, 1978.

Silverstein, Shel. *The Giving Tree.* Harper & Row, New York, 1964.

FILMSTRIPS

The Art of Pantomime in Church. Filmstrip with cassette soundtrack, script and reference guide. Features mime artist "Obie Good" (Randall Bane). This filmstrip will provide know-how, confidence and many ideas for pantomime sketches. In a workshop situation with two teens, he explains how to use hands, body and movement to interpret from the Bible. Psalm 150 is interpreted at the conclusion of the filmstrip. Available from Contemporary Drama Service, P.O. Box 7710, Colorado Springs, CO 80933, (303) 594-4422.

Be a Clown. Filmstrip, cassette soundtrack and reference guide. Professional clowns demonstrate the accepted traditions of clowning. Basic types of clowns are seen and defined. Costumes, actions and props are shown in action skits. The comic conventions of clowning are explained in detail with examples. This introduction to the art of clowning features clowns from Main Stage Productions. Available from Contemporary Drama Service.

Clowning for Kids. Filmstrip with cassette soundtrack and teacher's guide. 64 frames, 12 minutes. Shy kids, handicapped kids, noisy kids — clowning is for everybody. An informative filmstrip that shows and tells how any kid can discover the joy of being a clown. Available from Contemporary Drama Service.

An Introduction to Clown Ministry. 35mm filmstrip, color, 15 minutes in length, sound on one audio cassette, over 100 frames. Features Floyd Shaffer and presents the historical and biblical basis for clown ministry. Shows how Shaffer transforms a passive Sunday "audience" into a worshipping community for Christ. Available from Contemporary Drama Service.

An Introduction to Mime. 106-frame filmstrip with cassette soundtrack and script. Features Dr. E. Reid Gilbert (founder of the Valley Studio of Theatre Arts and nationally known mime), who explains and demonstrates the basics of mime. Movements of various parts of the body are seen in isolation with strobe photography. Available from Contemporary Drama Service.

Local Church Clown Ministry. Two 35mm filmstrips, soundtrack cassette and script. These filmstrips help a clown ministry group explain to new members what clown ministry is all about, and can also be a good resource to help interpret clown ministry to administrative bodies within the local church. The first filmstrip is entitled *Take Off Your Mask: An Introduction to Clown Make-up.* The second filmstrip is entitled *More Than a Clown,* and talks about how clown ministry got started, the rationale for clown ministry, and four ways clowning can be used in a local church. For information, write the United Methodist Film Service, 1525 McGavock St., Nashville, TN 37203.

The Mechanisms and Techniques of Mime. 129-frame filmstrip with cassette soundtrack and script. This filmstrip features Dr. E. Reid Gilbert, who explains the basic principles of mime action. Available from Contemporary Drama Service.

Put on a Happy Face. 35mm filmstrip, 52 frames, color, sound on audio cassette, work sheets. A professional clown shows how clown make-up is done. Close-up photography shows every step, from the first styling sketch to final powdering. Available from Contemporary Drama Service.

GAMES, ICE-BREAKERS, ETC.

Fluegelman, Andrew, ed. *The New Games Book: Play Hard, Play Fair, Nobody Hurt.* Doubleday, New York, 1976. A book of noncompetitive games that can be played by any number of people (two to 2,000) anywhere, and require no special equipment.

Ideas Books. A series of 21 (at this writing) volumes loaded with programming ideas, games, etc. Youth Specialties.

"Try This One." Regular feature of *GROUP Magazine.* Subscription Services: Box 202, Mt. Morris, IL 61054.

HISTORY

Towsen, John. *Clowns.* The Hawthorn Press, New York, 1978. Explores concept as it appears in all cultures, from Far Eastern to American Indian, throughout time (from B.C. to present).

JUGGLING

The Art of Juggling. 35mm filmstrip, 85 frames, color, sound on audio cassette. The Reverend Tom Woodward, who has taught more than 3,000 persons to juggle, explains and demonstrates the techniques and tricks. Manual frame advance allows for easy, individualized learning. Available from Contemporary Drama Service, P.O. Box 7710, Colorado Springs, CO 80933, (303) 594-4422.

Burgess, Hovey. *Circus Techniques.* Thomas Y. Crowell, New York, 1976. Covers juggling, equilibristics and vaulting.

Carlo. *The Juggle Book.* Random House, Westminster, Maryland, 1974. Basic how-to book on juggling.

Finnigan, Dave. *Joy of Juggling.* Juggle Bug, Edmonds, WA. Basic resource manual on juggling. Available from Juggle Bug, 23004 107th Place, West Edmonds, WA 98020.

MIME

Emerson, Elizabeth. "Mime with a Difference." *Theatrework Magazine*, March/April, 1983.

Gasiorowicz, Nina and Cathy. *The Mime Alphabet Book.* Lerner Publications Co., Minneapolis, MN, 1974.

Hamblin, Kay. *Mime: A Playbook of Silent Fantasy.* Doubleday, New York, 1978. This book is a basic introduction to mime. It is profusely illustrated with photographs and easy-to-follow instructions. Includes a collection of mime exercises.

Howard, Vernon. *Pantomimes, Charades and Skits.* Sterling Publishing Co., New York, 1959.

Kipnis, Claude. *The Mime Book.* Harper Colophone Books (Harper & Row), New York, 1974. This book includes chapters on isolation exercises, creating movement, and the mime of an object, and subject and object; and is a how-to book for those interested in improving or developing technique. A unique feature of the book is its "flip sequences," which are photographs that appear on the outer edges of the pages. When flipped, they produce visual mime sequences. Available from Contemporary Drama Service, P.O. Box 7710, Colorado Springs, CO 80933, (303) 594-4422.

Robb, Danni and Michael Sturko. *The Clown's Balloons, and Mime Sketches.* Five creative mime sketches for the beginning or accomplished mime. Each sketch is adaptable to the performer's skill level. Available from Contemporary Drama Service.

Stolzenberg, Mark. *Exploring Mime.* Sterling Publishing Co., New York, 1980. Available from Contemporary Drama Service.

Toomey, Susie Kelly. *Mime Ministry.* Contemporary Drama Service, Colorado Springs, CO, 1986. The first complete guidebook on Christian mime. Available from Contemporary Drama Service.

MOTION PICTURES

Annie Remembers. 16mm film, color, five minutes. This film is an excellent, but painful illustration of loneliness, aging and widowhood. A film by Kay Henderson based on a poem by Donna Swanson. Clowns like Bill "Diogenes" Peckham and Gary "Coco" Ramond use this as a basic resource in teaching clown ministry groups the importance of touch. Available from Mass Media Ministries, 2116 North Charles St., Baltimore, MD 21218, for purchase or rental.

*Clown. A story without words about a little boy and his faithful dog who live in the streets of Monmartre. The two become separated, and after a long search, the dog is finally found leading a blind man. Learning Co. of America, 1968.

*Clown of God. 10 minutes, color. Tomie de Paola's world-acclaimed picture-book version of the legend of the Little Juggler, translated into a heart-warming animated "children's" film. Weston Woods, 1982.

Juggler of Notre Dame. A film produced by Paulist Productions, CA. Story of a whiteface juggler who loses his desire to juggle after great personal tragedy, and then regains his faith.

The Juggling Lesson. 16mm film, color, 22 minutes. Produced by the Juggling Institute. Available through TAL Worldwide Productions, 717 Beverly Rd., Baltimore, MD 21222, (301) 285-4848. A street juggler and a juggling teacher lead a group through the five basic steps involved in learning to juggle.

MASS MEDIA MINISTRIES, 2116 North Charles St., Baltimore, MD 21218 (301) 727-3270. Film distributor and major rental source of 16mm films for use in the church. National source of Floyd Shaffer's contributions to the world of motion pictures, including the film, *The Mark of the Clown,* in which Socataco (Shaffer) and an entire congregation of clowns reenact the mysteries of faith, worship and ministry. Mass Media Ministries also handles the celebrative parable, *A Clown Is Born.* Write for information on clown ministry films.

*Note: These films are available in Suffolk County, Long Island, through the Suffolk Cooperative Library System and loaned through member libraries. Check local library systems to see if a similar lending cooperative is available.

Parable. 22 minutes, color. A whiteface clown joins a circus parade, takes upon himself the burdens of the lowly, the abused and the humiliated, and is rewarded with death in harness as a human marionette. Protestant Council of New York, 1964.

Peege. A young man accompanies his family to visit his dying grandmother in a nursing home. Peege (her nickname) has gone blind and lost some of her mental facilities. The visit is awkward because none of them knows how to deal with the unresponsive shell that was once a vibrant woman. When the others leave, the young man stays behind. He uses simple human touch and speaks to her softly of his early memories of her. He is able to communicate, and she knows that someone cares. Phoenix Films, 1974.

That's Life. 16mm color film, eight minutes. This film is a glance at the mystery and miracle of life by noted clown minister Floyd Shaffer. The film leads the viewer through the four seasons of the year. Available through Mass Media Ministries, 2116 N. Charles St., Baltimore, MD 21218.

ORGANIZATIONS

CLOWNS OF AMERICA, 2715 E. Fayette St., Baltimore, MD 21224. National organization for clowns with a number of "alleys" around the country.

FAITH AND FANTASY, Floyd Shaffer, 32185 Susilane, Roseville, MI 48066. This clown ministry organization was founded by Floyd Shaffer and has grown to include local clusters of Faith and Fantasy clowns all over the United States. Workshops are available.

FUNNY FARM CLOWNS, INC., Route 2, Box 170, Butler, GA 31006. Jim "Dune Buggy" Russell is a performing clown who does workshops on everything from make-up to magic. Funny Farm also has a thriving mail order business for persons who need clown supplies: make-up, balloons, magic tricks and the like. A catalog is available. Write for current cost information.

HOLY FOOLS CLOWN MINISTRY GROUP, Bill Peckham, Director, P.O. Box 1828, Springfield, IL 62705. National organization for local church clown groups. Over 500 affiliate groups around the country.

Note: These films are available in Suffolk County, Long Island, through the Suffolk Cooperative Library System and loaned through member libraries. Check local library systems to see if a similar lending cooperative is available.

JUGGLING INSTITUTE, 23004 107th Place West, Edmonds, WA 98020. Organization dedicated to teaching juggling techniques.

RINGLING BROTHERS AND BARNUM AND BAILEY COMBINED SHOWS, INC., Department of Educational Services, 1015 18th St. NW, Washington, D.C. 20036. Publishes a great deal of helpful material related to the circus. They have also prepared a unit of study entitled "Circus: A Teaching Unit." Bibliography from the unit is available separately and is extremely helpful.

SCHOOL FOR SILLIES, Box 13084, Wauwatosa, WI 53213. With Headmaster Bruce Clanton, School for Sillies is a sharing of celebratory worship ideas built around the church year. Clanton sends out an undetermined number of lessons each year — no fancy printing, just some good material in a celebratory mode. Though he doesn't deal with clowning as such, the material is generally excellent for clowns/ mimes who are exploring uses of their art in liturgy.

SISTER ADELAIDE ORTEGEL, SP., 2939 North 72nd Court, Apt. #1, Elmwood Park, IL 60635. Sister Adelaide is a clown, puppeteer and dancer who uses these three art forms in worship settings. She was a member of the Center for Contemporary Celebration, a group that developed worship services that include mime, dance or clowning, or can easily be adapted to include them. Write for workshops on liturgy and the arts.

WORKSHOP LIBRARY ON WORLD HUMOR, P.O. Box 23334, Washington, D.C. 20024, (212) 547-8055. Organization devoted to sharing information about uses of humor in the arts, sciences, professions and everyday living.

PERIODICALS

The Calliope. Official magazine of Clowns of America, 2715 E. Fayette St., Baltimore, MD 21224. The magazine is monthly and contains articles of general interest to clowns, including some how-to material. Advertisements keep you in touch with where you can locate costumes, clown shoes, make-up, magic paraphernalia, stunts and supplies.

Humor Events. Newsletter published by Workshop Library on World Humor, P.O. Box 23334, Washington, D.C. 20024.

Sourcemonthly: The Resource for Mimes, Clowns, Jugglers and Puppeteers. Magazine premiered in September, 1983. Includes a performance calendar each month, listing tours, international and national performance dates and festivals. For additional information, contact *Sourcemonthly*, ℅ Mimesource, Inc., P.O. Box 453, Times Square Station, New York, NY 10108.

SKITS, PLAYS AND ROUTINES

Brown, Margie. *Good News Caravan.* Clownabration, Dayton, OH. Collection of skits based on Bible stories for use by clowns. Available from Clownabration, 1810 Harvard Blvd., Dayton, OH 45406.

Hansen, Ruth. *The Christian Clown.* Contemporary Drama Service, Colorado Springs, CO, 1985. A performance kit of skits. Available from Contemporary Drama Service, P.O. Box 7710, Colorado Springs, CO 80933, (303) 594-4422.

Litherland, Janet. *Blessed Are the Peacemakers.* Contemporary Drama Service, Colorado Springs, CO, 1981. A one-act play for clown or mime performers tells a sentimental story woven into a fabric of warm laughter and symbolism. Four park clowns find the way to bring joy back into the lives of a kindly old birdman and a troubled teen-ager. Available from Contemporary Drama Service.

Litherland, Janet. *The Clown as Minister I and II.* Contemporary Drama Service, Colorado Springs, CO, 1980 and 1981. Two kits of workable skits and ideals for all age levels. Available from Contemporary Drama Service.

Litherland, Janet. *Scripture Skits for a Troupe of Clowns.* Contemporary Drama Service, Colorado Springs, CO, 1984. Several of the Bible's best-known teachings are included in a kit of 10 skits. Available from Contemporary Drama Service.

McVictor, Wes. *Clown Act Omnibus.* 3rd printing, 1978 (Magic, Inc., Chicago, 1970). Book includes over 200 workable clown acts for beginning, intermediate and advanced participants. Acts are classified by type, equipment needed, gymnastic skills required and practice required. Available from Contemporary Drama Service.

Mitchell, Jan. *Hallelujah! Amen!* Contemporary Drama Service, Colorado Springs, CO, 1981. A charming allegory for clown performers in a church setting. Easy to stage. Audience participation. Available from Contemporary Drama Service.

Moon, Clarice. *Here Come the Clowns.* Contemporary Drama Service, Colorado Springs, CO, 1976. Twenty action skits with how-to-do-it instructions. The playing time for each secular skit varies up to approximately 10 minutes. Available from Contemporary Drama Service.

Moynahan, Michael. *Come Passion. GROUP Magazine,* March, 1979. An easy-to-produce mime presentation that is a highly symbolic expression of the meaning of our relationship with Christ, and how that applies to our witness to others.

Sterelak, Richard and Marty Sherman. *Clown Hits and Skits.* Contemporary Drama Service, Colorado Springs, CO, 1981. A production-tested repertoire of clown skits. Five different styles of sketches are included — classic gags, dumb magic, tricks, caught-in-the-act and skits-with-props. This secular collection comes directly from the Main Stage Productions clown troupe repertoire. Twenty skits are included with prop diagrams and a booklet, "How to Write Your Own Clown Skits." Available from Contemporary Drama Service.

Toomey, Susie Kelly. *Clown Mimes for Christian Ministry.* Contemporary Drama Service, Colorado Springs, CO, 1984. Five thematic skits on a variety of Christian ideas. Available from Contemporary Drama Service.

Waters, Paul H. *The Clown's Bible.* Contemporary Drama Service, Colorado Springs, CO, 1983. Eight skits using mime and narrative for a troupe of six or more clowns. Subject: Bible stories. Available from Contemporary Drama Service.

SLIDES

Make-Up Training Slides. 51 slides, 30-minute tape, script. Demonstrates in detail the application of the three basic types of make-up for the clown whiteface, tramp and Auguste. Available from Clowns of America, Inc., P.O. Box 30, Eagleville, PA 19408.

APPENDIX

The following article originally appeared in the Long Island daily, *Newsday*, on Monday, August 16, 1982:

Clowns Put a New Face on Celebration of Mass
by LAURA DURKIN

On the altar of the church stands a priest. Dressed simply in white vestments with red circles, he lifts his arms in an open embrace and raises his head. It is the mask of death, or the whiteface clown.

Around him, a group of clowns dressed gaily in circus-bright costumes clasp their hands in the age-old symbol of prayer. Balloons bob from the pews, feather dusters fly as the flows cleanse the congregants in preparation for the liturgy.

"Let us pray," says the priest. This is the mass.

The scene is occurring at an increasing number of churches around the country. Spurred by church reforms and as an effort to reach parishioners in novel ways, clown ministers are springing up and spreading. They range from small groups that have grown up to hold formal "clown convocations," to articles in liturgical magazines to films by a Lutheran minister in Michigan who packages workshop kits for those who wish to be clowns.

On Long Island, clown ministry has a small but disparate membership, from mother-daughter teams in Nassau County to a 52-year-old sister of St. Joseph who wears whiteface clown make-up to teach religious education teachers how to celebrate by learning how to play.

It also has a devoted opposition, expressed in a running debate in the (Roman Catholic) Rockville Centre Diocese's weekly newspaper between people who support its symbolism and people who feel it degrades the purpose of liturgical worship.

While the clown ministry has reached Protestant denominations elsewhere, on Long Island, it has mostly been limited to the Catholic faith. Its impetus was Vatican II, when the Roman Catholic Church opened the doors to vernacular services and increased participation by the laity. But advocates say the clown ministry has historical precedent in the foundations of the church, among the medieval church festivals and the early "miracle plays."

The clowns wear the brightly colored costumes and make-up of circus characters and use simple props, such as balloons and feather dusters, to act out stories or parables from the Bible. During the mass, they mime the meaning of the spoken liturgy. At other occasions, such as during religious instruction classes, they act out skits and talk about the meaning of the parables they are performing.

On Long Island, there have been perhaps a half-dozen to a dozen clown masses, always held in addition to regular services, at churches such as St. Ignatius in Hicksville, and St. Mary of the Isle in Long Beach. More frequently, clowns have been used in classes for both children and adults.

The props the clowns use are symbols: balloons rise to heaven like incense; feather dusters are used to cleanse the congregation. Dennis Carter, a professional clown who leads a clown ministry in Hicksville, said that the whiteface, traditional make-up for mime, symbolizes the death of the ego.

Sister Regina McAuley's signature clown face is a small red heart and a blue cross on top of her whiteface, symbolizing the resurrection of Christ. "I get people to play, usually against their will, and then turn that around and have it become a prayer experience," she said.

Sister Regina, of the Sisters of St. Joseph, works in Brentwood, mostly with religious education teachers and parents of children who are going to make their first communion. She has been clowning for five years.

The Rev. Lawrence Penzes of St. Pius X parish in Plainview said that for the one clown mass he celebrated, he painted a small red cross on his forehead when he stood before the congregation, to indicate that he was entering into God's presence and love when he began the mass.

Penzes said most people are not ready for the clown liturgy and have to be educated about it first. But he added, "This is not circus clowning, but rather seeing Christ as a clown figure. Clowns are symbols of joy, symbols of hope. Christ was that. Clowns are nonconformist, and that's what Jesus was. Clowns are always very vulnerable. So was Jesus. Clowns are servant figures. Jesus was . . . someone who served."

But despite the clowns' sincerity, they have met with resistance within the body of the church. One member of the diocese wrote in *The Long Island Catholic*, "I'm not against being happy and joyous at mass, but the true happiness of the mass is in Jesus' acceptance of death for our sins and His glorious resurrection, not in clowns dancing around the altar. If you want to see clowns perform, go to the cirucs."

The Rev. John Gurrieri, of the Bishop's Committee on the Liturgy in Washington, D.C., said he found clowns at mass "personally insulting. I think it runs contrary to the liturgy, which is not theater. It's worship."

But Carter, who had fallen away from active church participation before discovering clowning about five years ago, said he can more easily express his love for other people while masked as a clown. "We can't pass on our love to other people as ourselves," he said. "In costume, we don't have to worry about our frail egos and pride." [1]

Stephen P. Perrone (left) and the Reverend James P. Spata

ABOUT THE AUTHORS

Stephen P. Perrone and the Reverend James P. Spata were introduced to clown ministry at a workshop given by Paul and Barbara Humphries at a youth leaders' convention in February, 1980. Soon afterward, Steve and Jim, along with a team of facilitators, gave their first clown workshop for Jim's youth group at Caroline Church (Episcopal) in Setauket, New York. Since then, they have given some 30 workshops — most on Long Island, but some as far away as New Mexico. Recently, they were invited to give their workshop at the same youth leaders' conference where they were introduced to clowning. Jim's clown troupe ministers regularly at several Long Island nursing homes, and makes special appearances at local hospitals, the Special Olympics and street fairs.

Stephen P. Perrone

Steve earned his bachelor's degree in speech and drama from Allegheny College in Meadville, Pennsylvania. Since then, he's been involved in drama in many forms.

During his two years of military service, he became involved in local civilian and military dramatics. He was part of the team that helped bring the Fourth Army Drama Contest award to Fort Sill, Oklahoma, for two consecutive years. He was cited for excellence in lighting design for Christopher Fry's *A Sleep of Prisoners,* and for lighting and set design for Arthur Miller's *All My Sons.*

Not one to just sit back in the church pew, he volunteered to organize a youth group in his parish in 1970. He joined the diocesan group, also. Currently, he is diocesan committee chairman, and serves on the board of managers for the diocesan youth center, Camp DeWolfe. An active member of his parish, he is a lay reader and chalice administrator, YPF advisor, acolyte coordinator and Sunday school teacher.

Steve is single and lives with his family in the suburban community of Dix Hills, about 35 miles east of Manhattan.

The Reverend James P. Spata

Jim, a secondary science teacher for the past 20 years, is a graduate of the State University of New York at Potsdam, with degrees in chemistry and education. He has done graduate work in marine science at C.W. Post College.

He began to get involved in youth ministry about 12 years ago as the adult advisor to a senior-high group and as a member of a ministry team at a state hospital youth facility. He attended the George Mercer School of Theology from 1976 to 1980, and was ordained deacon in 1981 and priest in 1983 by the Right Reverend Robert C. Witcher, Bishop of the Episcopal Diocese of Long Island.

Jim is a science teacher at Peconic Street Junior High School and serves as assistant to the rector at Caroline Church (Episcopal) in Setauket. He is the spiritual director of the Youth Ministries Committee of the Diocese of Long Island.

Jim is married, and he and his wife, Chris, have three children: Dawn, Stacey and Nickey. Jim and Chris recently celebrated their 20th wedding anniversary.

IF YOU ENJOYED
SEND IN HIS CLOWNS,
YOU WILL BE INSPIRED BY
THIS OTHER MERIWETHER PUBLISHING
CLOWN MINISTRY BOOK:

THE
CLOWN MINISTRY
HANDBOOK

by JANET LITHERLAND

You've read **Send in His Clowns**, and your group's had a successful clown ministry workshop. But you don't want to leave it at that — you're ready to go out and *minister*! **The Clown Ministry Handbook** will inspire you as it explains that clown ministry is not entertainment, not preaching in costume, but a means of touching souls. You'll find a wealth of details on clown types, make-up tricks, wardrobe and props, performance techniques, skits, gags and complete clown presentation scripts. You'll learn about the opportunities for outreach, clown ministry responsibilities and more. **The Clown Ministry Handbook** leads you through a poignant new way of practicing your faith — clown ministry! This paperback book is available at bookstores or from Meriwether Publishing Ltd., P.O. Box 7710, Colorado Springs, Colorado 80933.

NOTES: